Backgammon to Win

Chris Bray

For Gill & Kate

Acknowledgements

Firstly I must acknowledge the contribution made by my wife Gill, who over the years has painstakingly proof-read all of my work, correcting my many errors and making my prose intelligible. Without her, neither this book nor my previous works would have seen the light of day. I would also like to acknowledge the support I received from Gill and my daughter Kate whilst I wrote this book, sometimes at very strange hours of the day.

The original book was reviewed in great detail by my colleague Ray Kershaw and I am indebted to him for his many corrections and suggested improvements. Only he knows how many hours he spent checking diagrams, counting pips and shots and calculating percentages. This new edition was reviewed by Ray and also by Peter Bennet, one of the UK's top players, and I would like to thank them for their help and input. Any errors that remain are entirely my own.

My thanks to Richard Biddle for his excellent design work on the book's cover.

Finally, I would like to thank all the players who have wittingly, or unwittingly, contributed positions to this book. Without you, life would indeed be dull!

"We don't stop playing because we grow old, we grow old because we stop playing."

George Bernard Shaw

"The most exciting thing in life is winning and the second most exciting is losing."

Simon Barnes

"Backgammon, like love, like music has the power to make people happy."

Siegbert Tarrasch (paraphrased)

Contents

Chapter 1: Introduction

Why play backgammon? From a personal perspective I can easily answer that question. Back in the mid-1970s my only interest in games was in playing chess. By dint of a lot of study and little bit of natural talent I had become a competent player but never one who was going to set the world alight. Sometime around this period my girlfriend Gill, later to become my wife, had taught me to play backgammon. However, I hadn't shown any real interest, and had returned to the futile pursuit of chess playing excellence.

Then one night I was working through the small hours system testing some less than exciting software. In those days we were still using punched cards and everything took forever. To pass the time, one of the other analysts challenged me to a game of backgammon at fifty pence per point. Why not, I thought. Thirty minutes later I had lost £10 and realised that I knew absolutely nothing about the game.

That did it. All thoughts of chess were gone. I hate losing at anything but particularly when I don't know why I have lost. I was hooked by the game of backgammon and have remained so ever since. I long ago realised why I had lost in that first session, but I have continued the search for knowledge for the last thirty years and will probably do so for the next thirty as well.

In the meantime it has kept me amused, frustrated and intellectually challenged, probably in equal parts. It has given me some lifelong friendships and it has also managed to pay for the odd holiday or two over the years.

To provide a more general answer to the question of why we play backgammon, I think that the combination of skill and luck provides a perfect balance. In the short term a novice can beat a world champion but over the long haul the better player will win. The outrageous swings of fortune that can, and do, occur both frustrate us and excite us. They keep bringing us back for more of the same. Backgammon is also a supremely social game and it is a great way to meet new people and make friends whether that is over the board or on the Internet.

Although the popularity of backgammon faded in the late 1980s a core group of players, including myself, kept the game alive in the 'quiet years'. It is now undergoing a huge resurgence for a variety of reasons.

Firstly backgammon has not survived 5,000 years without good reason. It is a game that is easy to learn - you can become competent within six months - but it can take a lifetime to become a real expert. That fundamental challenge is true of all really good games and sports. Secondly the game flourishes when there is disposable income and leisure time available. Most backgammon is played for money and the more money there is, the more excitement is generated. Despite 9/11 and the War on Terror this century has seen economies improve and disposable incomes increase, although the current Eurozone crisis may give us a downturn in the short term.

However, there is one factor that dominates everything else when we look at the rise of backgammon and that is the Internet, and more particularly, broadband Internet. I have worked with computers all my life but the advent of mainstream Internet in 1997 (there was 1000% growth in the western world that year) is the single most influential event that I have seen in my lifetime.

In fifteen years the Internet has gone from quirky technology to something that provides the fundamental communications network of our world and which determines and influences much of our social interaction. Companies like Google have changed our lives forever and of one thing we can be sure – the pace of change will only accelerate.

In the world of gaming, whilst we were still paying to dial up to the Internet progress was slow as the costs outweighed the benefits. Early websites were very basic and in some cases very naïve – there were also many security issues. The arrival of broadband completely changed the economics – low-cost high-speed Internet was a different animal altogether and suddenly the world was a better place. People who previously had to travel thousands of miles to play games could now do so from the comfort of their own homes. The classic example is Jon Røyset of Norway who was World Champion in 2003. He lives just inside the Arctic Circle and did all of his training online before travelling to Monte Carlo to capture the game's ultimate crown.

Early Internet gambling was centred on slot machines and it became far too easy to get hooked. An ex-work colleague of mine got himself into £20,000 of debt and was just wondering how to explain this to his wife when with his last £300 of credit he won £70,000 in a single spin of the wheels and all his problems were solved – if only life were always that simple!

However, slot machines were mindless and the gambling community looked for something else. Coincidentally poker was already undergoing a resurgence in popularity because players had discovered the version of the game known as Hold'em. The combination of Hold'em and the Internet created a massive boom in online poker that is still continuing today. People who played a little poker for fun suddenly found they could earn their living at it and thus a new generation of players had arrived in a matter of two or three years.

Over the years I have played poker occasionally and enjoyed it, but it pales in comparison to backgammon. In poker there is a lot of dead time as you discard unplayable hands. There is no dead time in backgammon – you have to be constantly alert and each roll of the dice must be played to maximum effect. The swings of luck and fortune are outrageous but they make the game what it is. The social side of backgammon is also tremendous and some of my strongest friendships have been formed over the board. If you can't get an adrenalin rush from playing backgammon there is something seriously wrong with you.

These points have been well understood by the companies that run Internet poker and other game sites and they have been feverishly adding backgammon as an option. The number of online backgammon sites has mushroomed so that today's players are spoilt for choice. As popularity increases so does prize money and we can expect to see big money tournaments staged with increasing regularity. Typically we will see the same model that is used in poker with half the places in the final going to online qualifiers.

In conjunction with online play backgammon is finally benefitting from TV exposure. Media exposure is essential to the long term growth of the game and TV producers have begun to realise how exciting backgammon can be when well presented. The first programme of the modern era was the coverage of the 2005 World Championship final. It was superb and proved to be the catalyst for many more hours of TV coverage. This is set to increase in the future. I think we can safely say that backgammon is back from the 'quiet years'.

I have been the backgammon correspondent of 'The Independent' newspaper in the UK for the last eighteen years and hope to continue in that post for many more years to come. During that time I have published six books including this one.

With the current resurgence of interest in backgammon I felt that the time had come for me to write a new introduction to the game. This needed to take into account the many changes in theory that have happened in the last ten years because of the arrival of backgammon-playing computers. The so-called 'experts' of the 1970s would not last long against today's masters who have done much of their learning using modern neural net computer programmes with exotic names such as JellyFish, Snowie, gnubg and eXtreme Gammon. After computer analysis, one of the most highly acclaimed books of the 1970's was shown to have nearly 50% incorrect answers. That is not to denigrate the author - he was only working with the tools of his era - but it does show how much the game has moved on in the last thirty years.

I have laid this book out in a manner that will make learning the game as easy as it can ever be. As noted above, backgammon is apparently simple but actually quite complex and this book will only take you on the first part of your journey. You will have to study further material and play even more before you become an expert.

However, I hope that having set out on the right path your journey will be as straightforward as possible.

Addendum (June 2012)

Since I published the original version of this book in 2007 the western world's economies have gone through crisis. Although we are still feeling the effects of the recession, there are encouraging signs that the corner has been turned.

Backgammon has suffered from the recession and the subsequent lack of sponsors for tournaments and media coverage. It has also suffered from the US government's decision to bar its citizens from Internet gambling. The impact of this has been to remove thousands of potential players from online backgammon sites. There are now signs that this bar may not last too much longer which, if borne out, would be great for the game.

The most significant development in the game since the original book was published has been the emergence of eXtreme Gammon (XG) as the strongest backgammon computer program in the world. XG has had a tremendous impact on the theory of the game as we will witness in subsequent chapters.

For this new edition I have checked all of my solutions using eXtreme Gammon and this has resulted in some minor changes to the original text. I have added a new chapter describing how to respond to the opening roll and there have been substantial revisions to the chapters on computers (not surprisingly) and online play.

Chapter 2: A Short History

Backgammon is one of the oldest games in existence alongside Go and Chess. It is probably about 5,000 years old and may well have originated in the region known today as Iraq. An excellent pictorial history of the game can be found in Jacoby & Crawford's "The Backgammon Book".

The board with its twenty-four points has been around for a long time but the game has not always been called backgammon. Early forerunners of today's game were called Senet and Mancala. The Romans were the first to make it truly popular with their version called "Duodecum Scripta et Tabulae" or "Tables" for short.

Frescoes in many a Roman villa depict the game in progress (the players were not always completely clothed!). The Emperor Claudius was a keen player – he had a special board built on the back of his chariot – and Nero played for today's equivalent of $10,000 a game.

It became so popular during the Crusades that soldiers below a certain rank were banned from playing. It is mentioned in early literature, both in Chaucer's Canterbury Tales and by Shakespeare in Love's Labour's Lost –

> "This is the ape of the form,
> monsieur the Nice,
> that, when he plays at **tables**,
> chides the dice,
> in honourable terms."

No one knows for sure where the name came from - the word backgammon first appeared in print in 1645 - but most likely it comes from the Middle English baec = back and gamen = game.

Backgammon appears consistently in art throughout the second millennium, most famously in "The Garden of Earthly Delights" by Hieronymus Bosch and "The Triumph of Death" by Pieter Brueghel.

The game has long been popular in the Middle East and visitors to that region will be familiar with the clack-clack of checkers being moved on wooden boards at the many street-side cafes. Players in the Middle East still do not use the doubling cube so that has created a gulf between western and eastern players that is seldom bridged.

The game was also played in the west throughout the last three centuries of the second millennium but it had constant battles with the clergy and the authorities who wanted to ban it because of the gambling element – not too dissimilar to some areas of the world today!

Its popularity continued through Victorian times - it was very popular at country house weekend parties - but it wasn't until the introduction of doubling that backgammon really became popular.

By the 1920s it was losing its appeal in the fast-paced society of the day because each game took too long and it was difficult to wager large amounts of money. Then, around 1925-6, some genius (or possibly several of them) in either New York or Boston came up with the idea of doubling.

At a stroke it solved the problems of the day and introduced a whole new level of skill that wasn't immediately understood at the time, and indeed is still not fully understood today. Of the many backgammon books that have been written, only four of them are wholly devoted to doubling and only two of those can be recommended as further reading material. We shall look at doubling in detail in Chapters 8 and 10.

The game flourished in the US and the UK until the Wall Street crash of 1929 removed the availability of ready cash and once again the dice cups went silent.

From 1930 to the mid-1960s the game entered a fallow period. No books were written, the players disappeared and the only sign of the game was as a prop in the occasional advertisement. Throughout the twentieth century backgammon could quite often be seen in adverts, normally in support of a relaxed and affluent lifestyle.

As we noted in the Introduction, backgammon seems to flourish when there is disposable income and in the 1970s the advent of oil money saw a huge resurgence in its popularity. Prince Alexis Obolensky, exiled from Russia, created the international backgammon tournament circuit that flourishes to this day and big money events attended by celebrities became the norm. James Hunt, Jackie Stewart, Hugh Hefner, Lucille Ball, Omar Sharif and many other high-flyers were to be seen at the tables. Jimmy Connors whiled away dead time at Wimbledon with his backgammon board.

Probably the most famous (or infamous) of them all was Lord Lucan and, but for backgammon, the tragic sequence of events that culminated with the murder of his nanny may never have happened. "Lucky" Lucan became a full time gambler after a particularly good run at backgammon. In truth he was just an average player and never cut out to be a professional gambler. His legacy was to have a particular move, "The Full Lucan", named after him.

In the 1980s and early 1990s a group of strong players, including US experts Paul Magriel and Bill Robertie, worked hard to gain a better understanding of the game. Books began to appear on backgammon theory but progress was relatively slow.

The real advances in theory and playing practice came with computers and particularly with the application of neural network technology. After pioneering work by Dr. Gerry Tesauro in the IBM Laboratories in White Plains, New York, two commercial programs, JellyFish and Snowie, dominated the market in the early years of the new century. A third program, gnubg, which is free, also become available. Three years ago we saw the emergence of eXtreme Gammon which is now the strongest backgammon-playing computer program in the world. We shall discuss these programs in more detail in later chapters.

Chapter 3: The Basic Rules of Play

Setting up the Board

The diagram below shows the backgammon board set up ready for play. Each player has five checkers on his 6-point, three checkers on his 8-point, five checkers on his 13-point and two checkers on his 24-point. A player's 6-point and 8-point will always be on the near side of the board and the 13- and 24-points will always be on the far side. From the point of view of the opposing side the point numbers are reversed. Your 13-point is your opponent's 12-point, your 3-point his 22-point, etc.

Black is moving his checkers anticlockwise and White is moving his clockwise.

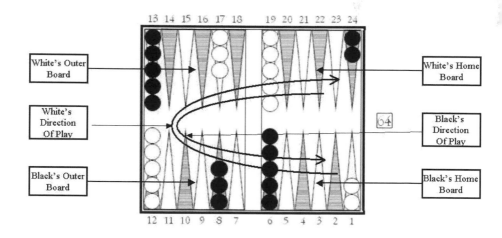

The board can also be set up as a mirror image of the above as follows:

9

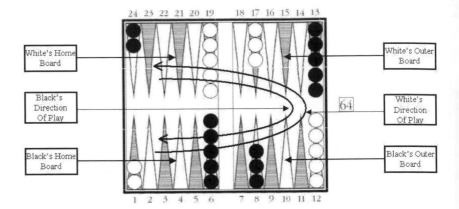

Now Black's home board is in the bottom left hand corner and he will be moving his checkers clockwise while White moves anticlockwise. When first learning to play, most people are more comfortable with one set-up rather than the other but you must get used to both. After a little practice it becomes second nature to play either way. In the past the board was always set up with the home boards nearer to the source of light – hopefully that is not an issue in the 21st century.

Object of the Game

The object of the game is for each player to bring all his checkers into his home board, and then to bear them off the board. The first player to get all his checkers off the board is the winner.

Equipment

Now let's look at the equipment you need to play backgammon.

Backgammon Board

As shown above, backgammon is played on a board consisting of twenty-four narrow triangles called points. The triangles alternate in colour and are grouped into four quadrants of six triangles each. The quadrants are referred to as the player's home board and outer board and the opponent's home board and outer board. The home and outer boards are separated from each other by a ridge down the centre of the board called the bar.

Checkers (Men)

Thirty round stones, fifteen each of two different colours, generally referred to as checkers in the US but often called men in the UK. I will use the term checkers throughout this book.

Dice

Six-sided dice, numbered from 1 to 6. For convenience, two pairs of dice, one pair for each player, are generally used. Precision dice (commonly used in casinos), specially machined for fair rolls, should be used if possible.

Dice Cups

Used to shake and throw the dice. Again, each player has his own dice cup. The best cups have a ridge just below the lip on the inside of the cup to ensure fair rolling. Some clubs use baffle boxes, a device through which the dice are cast, to reduce even further the chance of a player "interfering" with the dice.

Doubling Cube

A six-sided die, marked with the numerals 2, 4, 8, 16, 32 and 64. This is used to keep track of the number of points at stake in each game as well as to indicate which player last doubled. (You will occasionally find a doubling cube marked with a 1 instead of 64.) At the start of the game the doubling cube is set with the 64 (64 equates to 1) face uppermost and is placed to one side of the board, centrally between the players as shown in the diagrams above.

Notation

There was no agreed notation for recording games and moves for many years. In the 1970s a standard notation was finally adopted and I will be using that notation throughout this book.

Dice rolls are given as two numbers followed by a colon. The numbering of points is based on the point of view of the player whose turn it is to move. Each point therefore has two numbers, depending on who is on roll. White's 5-point is Black's 20-point. Diagrams are normally numbered from the viewpoint of the player whose home board is at the bottom of the diagram; in the diagrams above that is Black. Each movement is shown by giving the start and end point of the checker separated by a '/'. If a player is on the bar and fails to enter, a 0 is used to represent his roll (sometimes the word fan is used). If a player is on the bar against a closed board (his opponent owns all six of his home board points), his move is left blank or notated 'no play'.

Hits are indicated by an asterisk (*) – hitting will be explained below. A move made from the bar has 'bar' as its starting point. A move bearing off a checker has 'off' as its ending point. Where more than one checker is moved identically, as is often the case with doubles, this fact is indicated by showing the number of checkers moved in brackets after the move. All moves in a game are numbered.

The doubling cube is indicated by a square outline on the right-hand side of the board. If Black owns the cube it is shown at the lower right; if White owns it, it is shown at the upper right. The value of the cube is always shown within this square.

Here is the shortest possible backgammon game, one of only two moves:

BLACK	WHITE
1. 62: 24/18, 13/11	1. 55: 8/3(2), 6/1(2)*
2. 63: 0	2. Double
3. Drop	

The plays in this simple game will become clearer once we have studied the basics of play. When using a diagram to discuss a single move, the dice roll is shown within the diagram. For example for the first move of the game above we would use the following diagram:

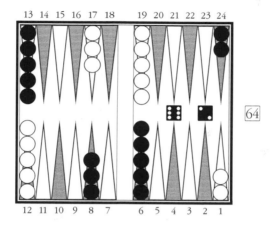

The fact that the dice are shown in black indicates that it is Black's turn and he must decide how to play this roll of 62. Throughout this book, unless explicitly stated otherwise, it is Black's turn to play.

Playing the Game

Starting the Game Each player rolls one die. The player with the higher number makes the first move, using the number from his die and that from his opponent's. In the event that both players roll the same number, each re-rolls to determine who makes the first move. In the event of subsequent ties this process is repeated until the dice show different numbers.

13

Automatic Double If both players roll the same number they can agree to double the stakes – this is called an automatic double. It is normal to limit automatics to one per game.

Rolling the Dice The players throw the dice alternately throughout the game, except in the case where a player cannot make a legal move and therefore forfeits his turn (note that he may still use the doubling cube even if he cannot move). The roll of the dice indicates how many pips (a pip is the distance between two adjacent points on the board) the player is to move his checkers. If the same number appears on both dice, for example 44 or 66 (called a double) the player is entitled to four moves instead of two. Thus if he rolls 55 he can move up to four checkers, but each move must consist of five pips.

Rules of Rolling

These are the commonly accepted rules of rolling:

- The dice must be rolled together and land flat on the surface of the right-hand section of the board, from the point of view of the roller. The player must re-roll both dice if either die lands outside the right-hand board, lands on a checker or does not land flat (known as cocked dice).

- A turn is completed when a player picks up his dice. If the play is incomplete or otherwise illegal, the opponent has the option of accepting the play or requiring the player to make a legal play. A play is deemed to have been accepted as made when the opponent rolls his dice or offers a double to start his own turn. Some clubs play what is called 'legal plays'. This means that if an illegal move has been made it MUST be corrected.

- If a player rolls his dice before his opponent has completed his turn by picking up his dice, the player's roll is voided. This rule is generally waived any time a play is forced or when there is no further contact between the opposing forces. Again some clubs play that premature rolls stand and you can take advantage of your opponent's mistake, knowing what his roll will be.

14

Moving the Checkers

Each player's turn begins with the roll of both his dice. He then moves one or more of his checkers in accordance with the numbers on the dice. The numbers on the two dice constitute separate moves. For example, if a player rolls a 4 and 6, he may move one checker four pips to an open point (one that is not occupied by two or more opposing checkers) and another checker six pips to an open point or he may move one checker ten pips to an open point, but only if one of the intermediate points (either 4 or 6 pips from the starting point) is also open. The bar is not counted as a point on the board.

The checkers are always moved around the board from the opponent's home board towards the player's home board. The two checkers on his 24-pt have the furthest distance to travel, whilst the other checkers have shorter journeys to make. A player's checkers move in the opposite direction to those of his opponent; that is, each player moves his checkers from his own higher-numbered points to his lower-numbered points.

A checker may only be moved to an open point. A checker may move to a point if it is occupied by only one of the opponent's checkers. In this case the opposing checker is "hit" and placed on the bar - see "Hitting and Entering" below. As an example of a simple move let us assume that Black has a 53 to play in the opening position shown below:

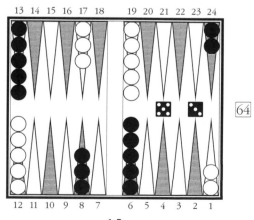

He cannot move a checker 24/19 with the 5 because White "owns" that point (he has two or more checkers on it) but he could move 24/21 with the 3 because that point is vacant. Thus Black could, if he so wished, play 24/21/16 but he could not move 24/19/16.

To avoid single checkers (known as blots) becoming vulnerable to being hit, a player can try to use his roll to "make a point". A player "makes a point" by positioning two or more of his checkers on it. He then "owns" that point, and his opponent cannot move a checker to that point nor touch down on it when taking the combined total of his dice with one checker.

To return to our example of Black to play 53 as his opening roll, the best move is actually 8/3, 6/3. Black then has two checkers on his 3-point and owns that point until such time as he should choose to move one or both checkers again.

If a player makes six points in a row he has completed a prime. Creating a six-point prime means that an opposing checker cannot move past, since it cannot be moved more than six pips at a time – the largest number on one die. A six-point prime is ideal but shorter primes, i.e. four- or five-point primes are also very powerful.

A player must use both numbers of a roll if it is legally possible to do so (or all four numbers of a double). When only one number can be played, the player must play that number. If either number can be moved but not both, the larger number must be played. When neither number can be played, the player loses his turn. In the case of doubles, when fewer than four numbers can be played, as many numbers as possible must be played.

Hitting and Entering As noted above, a single checker on a point is called a blot. If you move a checker on to an opponent's blot, or touch down on it in the process of moving the combined total of your roll, the blot is hit, placed on the bar and must re-enter into your home board. A player may not make any other move until he has brought the checker on the bar back into play.

Re-entry is made on a point equivalent to the number of one of the dice cast, providing the point is not owned by the opponent (occupied by two or more of his checkers). For example, if a player rolls 4 and 5, he may enter a checker on either the opponent's 4-pt or his 5-pt, so long as it is open.

If neither point is open, the player loses his turn. In the case where a player has more than one checker on the bar, he must enter as many as he can and then forfeit the remainder of his turn if any checkers remain on the bar. After the last of his checkers has been entered, any unused numbers on the dice must be played, by moving either a checker that has entered or another checker.

A player who has made all six points in his home board is said to have a closed board. If the opponent then has any checkers on the bar he will not be able to re-enter them. The opponent therefore forfeits his roll, and will continue to do so until the player opens a point in his home board, thus providing a point of entry.

Note that whilst a player may forfeit his roll he never forfeits his right to double at the start of each turn, should he have access to the doubling cube.

Bearing Off Once a player has moved all fifteen of his checkers into his home board, he may commence "bearing off". A player bears off a checker by rolling a number that corresponds to the point on which the checker resides, and then removing the checker from the board. Thus, rolling a 4 permits the player to remove a checker from the four-point. Checkers borne off the board never re-enter play. The player who bears all his checkers off first wins the game.

A player may not bear off checkers while he has a checker on the bar or outside his home board. Thus if, in the process of bearing off, a player leaves a blot which is hit by his opponent, he must first re-enter the checker in his opponent's home board, and bring it back around the board to his own home board before he can recommence the bearing off process.

17

In bearing off, a player must remove checkers from points corresponding to the numbers rolled on the dice. However, in certain cases, he may elect not to bear off a checker. He may instead, if he can, move a checker inside his home board a number of pips equivalent to the number(s) on the dice. If the player rolls a number higher than the highest point on which he has a checker, he must bear off a checker from the highest occupied point.

Thus if he rolls 63 and his 6-pt has already been cleared but he has checkers on his 5-pt, he may use the 6 to remove a checker from the 5-pt. The rules require that a player must use both numbers of his roll (all four in the case of a double) if possible. If he can make moves that don't involve bearing off, he is free to do so. Otherwise he must bear off if that is the only legal play.

Note also that whilst the rules require that both numbers must be played if at all possible, the numbers may be played in either order. As an example look at the following position:

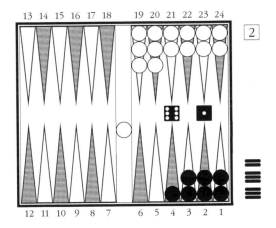

Black has already borne off eight checkers (indicated in the diagram by the eight Black discs to the right hand side of the board). With this 61 Black can choose between several legal plays including 4/off, 1/off, leaving a blot that could be hit by White's checker that is still on the bar, or 4/3, 3/off leaving no blots. Obviously the latter is to be preferred.

18

Winning the Game The player who bears all his checkers off first wins the game. You can win a single game, a gammon or a backgammon. If your opponent has already borne off one or more of his checkers when you bear off your last checker you win a single game. If you bear off all your checkers before your opponent has borne off a single checker then you win a gammon and twice the stake. If you bear off all your checkers before your opponent has borne off any of his and he still has a checker either in your home board or on the bar then you win a backgammon and triple the stake.

Types of Play

There are three basic types of backgammon play:

Money (head-to-head)

Most backgammon is played for a meaningful stake. It is possible to play purely for fun but the doubling cube introduces a factor that makes it more difficult to play without a stake.

In a money game at the start of play the two players agree a basic stake, let us say £1 per point. If a player wins a single game he wins 1 point; if he wins a gammon he wins two points, that is £2, and if he wins a backgammon he wins three points (£3).

These basic win rates are always multiplied by the value of the doubling cube. If for example the doubling cube is on 4 when the game ends and the winning player has won a gammon then he wins 8 points (4x2). You can see how the doubling cube can quickly help you to generate large wins (or losses).

Money (Chouette)

When you first play backgammon you are likely to play against one other person, be that your spouse, friend or teacher. However, backgammon is by its nature a very social game and, shortly after the invention of the doubling cube in the 1920s, a multi-player version was invented.

This was called 'Chouette' in which any number of people, normally between three and eight, take part in the same game.

This version of the game, which is the most exciting and also the most instructive, is described in Chapter 12.

Tournament (Match) play

In match or tournament play the two players agree to play to a fixed number of points. For example, a seven point match is won by the first person to score seven points where the nominal stake in each game is 1 point and the doubling cube and type of win are applied as before. In our example above, if a player won 8 points in the first game of a seven point match he would win the match immediately because 8 is one more than he needs to win. We shall cover tournament play in Chapter 13.

Now that we have covered the all the basic rules, let's see how they would be applied in a real game.

Chapter 4: A Sample Game

During this game I shall show the board position every so often but not after every play. Each diagram reflects the position after the moves that precede it. To get the best out of this chapter I suggest that you get out your own board and follow the moves one by one. I shall keep the comments relatively brief - the idea here is to get you familiar with the notation and to clarify the rules set out in the preceding chapter. Note that we will not be using the doubling cube in this game.

BLACK	WHITE
1. 31: 8/5, 6/5	
The best opening roll. Black makes his own 5-pt.	
	1. 64: 24/18/14
	White tries to escape one of his two rearmost checkers. Notice that the 18-pt had to be open so that he could make this play.

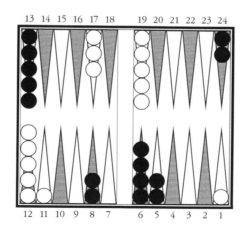

2. 42: 13/9, 13/11*

Black hits the White blot on his 11-pt and sends it to the bar. Notice the asterisk with 13/11 designates the hit. White must now re-enter this checker before he can move any other checkers.

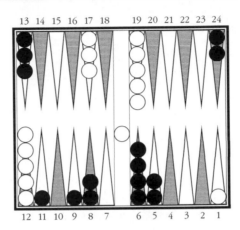

2. 61: bar/24/18

White enters his checker with the 1 – notice that he couldn't use the 6 to enter because Black owns that point – and then again attempts to move a back checker towards home by playing 24/18.

3. 62: 13/7*, 9/7

Black puts White back on the bar by hitting 13/7* and with the second half of his move completes his 7-pt. The 7-pt is commonly known as the bar-point. Black now has four points in a row, his 5, 6, 7 and 8-pts. This is known as a four-point prime.

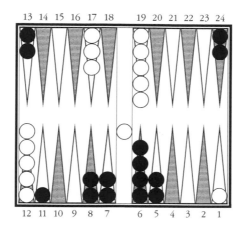

3. 65: 0

White fails to enter from the bar because both the 6-pt and 5-pt are owned by Black. He therefore forfeits his turn.

4. 44: 24/20(2), 8/4(2)

Black rolls double 4. Remember he has four 4's to play. With the first two fours he advances his back checkers together and with the other two fours he makes a new home board point, his 4-pt, by moving 8/4(2).

4. 51: bar/24, 13/8

White enters his checker from the bar and plays the 5 safely by moving 13/8, i.e. he moves a checker from one point that he owns (his 13-pt, better known as the mid-point) to another point that he owns, his 8-pt.

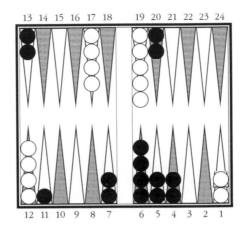

5. 66: 20/8(2)	
The biggest roll in backgammon allowing Black to advance 24 pips in a single roll. He brings both checkers from his 20-pt to his 8-pt.	
	5. 33: 8/5(2), 6/3(2)
	White responds with his own double and uses it to make two new home board points.
6. 65: 13/7, 13/8	
Black brings the last two checkers from his mid-point to the safety of his 7- and 8-pts. Note he already owned those two points.	
	6. 42: 8/4, 6/4
	White makes another home board point.
7. 54: 8/3, 7/3	
And Black responds by making another of his own – he now has a full prime of six consecutive points.	

7. 61: 13/7, 8/7

White makes his bar-point. He now has his own five-point prime from his bar-point to his 3-pt. The problem is that he does not have any enemy checkers trapped behind it.

8. 22: 6/2(2)

Another double! Black now has a seven-point prime.

8. 65: 13/7, 13/8

White moves two checkers down from his mid-point.

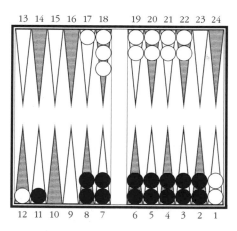

9. 62: 11/5, 8/6

Before he can bear any checkers off they must all be in his home board so Black begins to move the last five checkers into his home board.

9. 65: 8/2, 7/2

White continues to build his home board and forms a full (six-point) prime.

10. 66: 8/2

Black rolls double sixes but can play only one of them moving 8/2. He can't move the checkers on his bar-point because White owns his 1-pt. He therefore forfeits his other three sixes.

10. 62: 13/5

White brings his last checker from the mid-point into his home board.

11. 55: 7/2(2), 5/off(2)

Disaster strikes. With his first two fives Black brings his last two checkers 'home' and then with his other two fives he bears two checkers off the board. This leaves a blot (a single checker) exposed on his 5-pt. If White can roll a 4 he will be winning.

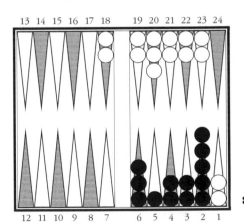

11. 55: 7/2(2), 6/1(2)

No luck. White misses the shot and has to damage his home board.

12. 65: 6/off, 5/off

Two more checkers safely off.

12. 55: No play

White cannot move a five legally anywhere on the board so must forfeit his turn.

13. 61: 6/off, 6/5

Another checker off but another blot is left.

13. 65: 24/18/13

Again no luck. White runs one back checker and hopes to save the gammon.

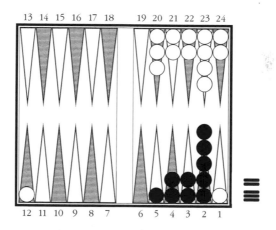

14. 51: 5/4, 4/off

Remember Black can play his dice rolls in any order. Here he deliberately plays the 1 first so that he can then play 4/off with the 5. Notice that if he plays 5/off with the 5 then any play of the 1 will leave a blot.

	14. 62: 13/5
	Still trying to save the gammon.
15. 43: 4/off, 4/1*	
Black is forced to leave another shot.	
	15. 31: bar/24*/21
	Finally, White hits – but is it too late?

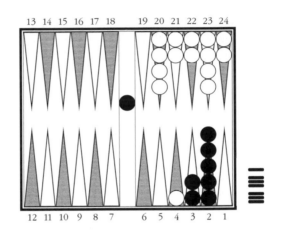

16. 54: No play	
Black cannot enter because white owns both his 5-pt and his 4-pt.	
	16. 64: 21/11
	White runs for home
17. 43: No Play	
	17. 66: 11/5, 5/off(3)
	White brings his last checker home with 11/5 and then because he has no checkers on his 6-pt bears three checkers off his 5-pt.

18. 62: bar/19/17

Black enters from the bar and makes a run for it. Note that he cannot bear off a checker with the 2 because not all his checkers are in his home board.

18. 61: 5/off, 1/off

19. 53: 17/9

This is going to be close.

19. 52: 5/off, 2/off

20. 61: 9/3, 2/1

Black brings his straggler home at last but doesn't have a checker on the 1-pt to take off so he 'unstacks' his overburdened 2-pt, a good idea in endings.

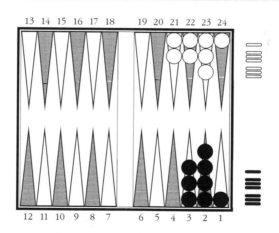

	20. 61: 4/off, 1/off
21: 65: 3/off(2)	**21. 43: 4/off, 3/off**
22. 62: 3/off, 2/off	**22. 52: 3/off, 2/off**
23. 63: 2/off(2)	

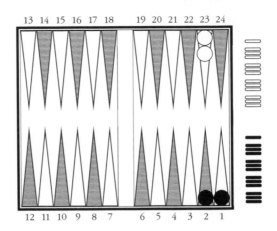

13 14 15 16 17 18   19 20 21 22 23 24

12 11 10 9 8 7   6 5 4 3 2 1

And so, as often happens in backgammon, the result is in doubt until the very end of the game. Any roll by White that doesn't contain a 1 will win for him and even double 1's is OK but he rolls....

23: 41: 2/off, 2/1

24. 32: 2/off, 1/off and wins

I hope that this sample game has given you a good idea of backgammon in practice. It should also give you some idea of how exciting the game can be and the kind of turnarounds that can happen.

For most of the game White was the distinct underdog and yet he came within a whisker of winning it – only bad luck on the last roll where he was a heavy favourite (as we shall see in a subsequent chapter) prevented him from triumphing.

Chapter 5: The Opening Roll

Basic Strategy

In this chapter we are going to examine how to play the opening rolls. As with other games such as chess the opening roll goes a long way towards defining the type of game that will evolve. Understanding how to play the opening rolls and the reasons for making the recommended plays will help you to develop your game considerably.

In chess, there are passive openings, for example the Caro-Kann, and active openings, such as the Sicilian. In backgammon we will see that certain opening rolls can be played aggressively or passively and that there are certain situations when one is to be preferred over the other.

So what are our objectives in the opening? Backgammon is primarily a race but if racing were the only goal nobody would play it. Whilst in the end the race will determine the winner, there are many other plots and sub-plots within a game. To enable us to race effectively we need to create safe landing places for our checkers, that is, make points. We also need to do as much as possible to hinder our opponent's moves. Ideally we would like to trap one or more of his checkers behind a strong blockade. We do this by building a prime - a set of contiguous points - where the ultimate is a full prime of six points in a row. Whilst six is ideal five-point and four-point primes are also very strong.

So we set out to a) create new points – preferably those that easily form part of a prime and b) begin to race for home. With regard to the second objective the most difficult checkers to get home are the two furthest away at the start of the game. Those are the two checkers on our opponent's ace-point (our 24-pt). It therefore makes sense in the opening to give those checkers high priority. A third objective is to unstack our heavy points. In the starting position we have five checkers on both our mid-point (13-pt) and our 6-pt. Five checkers on a point is inefficient so we want to redistribute those checkers as quickly as we can.

It is not always possible (or desirable) to move checkers to a safe landing point. Remember that a checker on its own is called a blot and that a blot, when hit, must re-enter from the bar. In the opening we typically see two sorts of blots:

- Builder - a blot that can be used next roll (if left unmolested) to help make (with another checker) a new point.

- Slot - a deliberately bold attempt to create a new point by exposing a blot close to your opponent's attackers with the hope of covering it with another checker next turn to create a new point.

Backgammon is a game of risk and reward and the opening is the ideal time to take a balanced risk in order to improve your position. This is because both home boards are undeveloped at the start of the game so that any blots that get hit can easily re-enter.

Now we will look at the possible rolls of the two dice. Imagine one die is blue and the other is red. There are 36 possible rolls of the two dice as shown in the table below. The numbers on the blue die are shown in bold italics:

Dice	1	2	3	4	5	6
1	*1*1	*12*	*13*	*14*	*15*	*16*
2	*2*1	*22*	*23*	*24*	*25*	*26*
3	*3*1	*32*	*33*	*34*	*35*	*36*
4	*4*1	*42*	*43*	*44*	*45*	*46*
5	*5*1	*52*	*53*	*54*	*55*	*56*
6	*6*1	*62*	*63*	*64*	*65*	*66*

Each of the six doubles occurs once and each of the non-doubles occurs twice. For example, 31 can be thrown as a *3* on the blue die and a 1 on the red die or as a *1* on the blue die and a 3 on the red die.

If we exclude the doubles – as you can never open with a double – then there are actually only 15 opening rolls to consider. These 15 rolls fall neatly into four groups:

Rolls that are always played the same way (5): **31, 42, 53, 61, 65**
Rolls on which there is broad agreement (2): **63, 62**
Split or slot rolls (3): **21, 41, 51**
Rolls with no broad agreement (5): **52, 54, 64, 43, 32**

It is perhaps surprising that after 5,000 years of play we still can't agree on how to play some of the opening rolls!

Rolls Always Played the Same Way

These five rolls are the best you can have because they give you an immediate solid asset. Four of them create a new point whilst the fifth gets one of the back checkers safely to the mid-point (your 13-pt)

31

The strongest roll of all is 31. This allows you to make your 5-pt by playing 8/5, 6/5 as shown below:

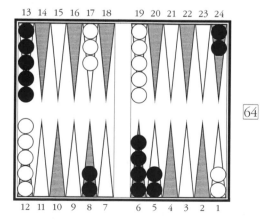

Of all the points on the board the two most important at the start of the game that you should strive to make are your own 5-pt and your opponent's 5-pt (your 20-pt). Long ago, Paul Magriel, one of the world's finest players and certainly the best author/teacher for many years, coined the term 'Golden Point' for the 5-pt to reflect its importance and the name has stuck.

Why is it so important? It is a new point in your home board which will hamper your opponent's entry should you hit one of his checkers. Most importantly it forms the third point in a potential prime – all you need now is to make your bar-point (your 7-pt) to create a four-point prime.

42

The next best roll is 42 which is played 8/4, 6/4 to make your 4-pt as shown here:

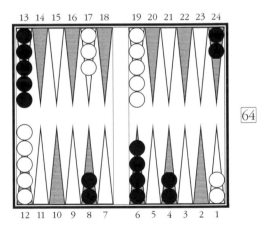

Magriel named this the 'Silver Point'. Whilst not quite as strong as the 5-pt it is still a powerful point to make and 42 is the second best opening roll.

The reason it is not as strong as 31 is the 'gap' between the 4-pt and the 6-pt. If you subsequently make your 5-pt you will have a very powerful position but if your opponent makes it he will have a strong defence.

53

The third opening roll that makes a home board point is 53. It is played 8/3, 5/3 as shown:

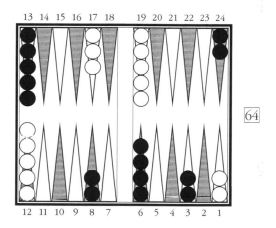

Any new point is an improvement and making the 3-pt is still a good start to the game. It is not as good as the 5-pt or 4-pt because there is now a 'double gap' between the new point and the 6-pt.

Back in the 1970s 53 was played 13/8, 13/10 because it was felt that the 3-pt was too deep a point to make on the first roll of the game. However, Jason Lester switched to making his 3-pt and noted that he was winning more games with this play. Soon all the budding New York professionals followed suit. Nowadays making the 3-pt is universal.

61

The last of the point making rolls is 61, played 13/7, 8/7:

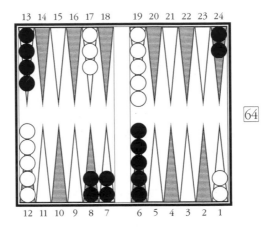

Beginners often think that making the bar-point is better than making the 5-pt but it is not, for a number of reasons. Firstly all home board points are useful because they limit your opponent's entering numbers when you hit one of his checkers. Making the bar-point does not do anything to stop your opponent entering from the bar.

Secondly, the most difficult checkers to activate from the opening position are the five checkers on your 6-pt because they have so few possible destinations. Rolls of 31, 42 and 53 all make use of one of those checkers but 61 does not. Whilst 61 is definitely a good roll the structure that it leaves is not as good as after one of the other three rolls. On the up side it does create a three-point prime that can be extended in either direction.

65

The last of our 'forced' opening rolls is 65 which is played 24/13:

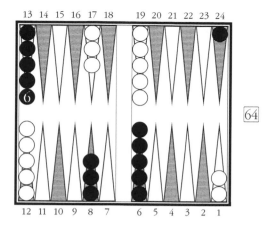

This is a good roll because it gets one of the two back checkers halfway home in complete safety. The move is known as 'Lover's Leap'. Once you have started with a 65 you have a fairly straightforward game plan presented to you – run the other checker out as quickly as you can. Note that in diagrams we insert a number in the fifth checker when there are more than five checkers on a point.

For many years it was not appreciated how powerful it is to escape one checker completely so early in the game. It is far easier to escape one checker than two and to have 50% of the job done on the first move is a distinct advantage.

Rolls on Which There is Broad Agreement

These two rolls are 63 and 62 and the same theory applies to each of them, although with 62 there is an (old-fashioned) additional option.

63

There are two options with this play. The first is 24/18, 13/10 as shown below:

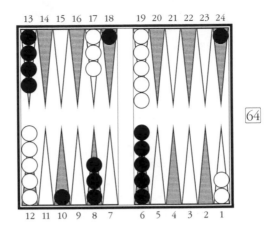

The thinking behind this play is twofold. Let us consider the first part of the move, the six, played 24/18. Firstly it attempts to make the opponent's bar-point by slotting it. If White doesn't hit the blot then Black will be nearly even money to make the point on his next turn.

Secondly the play may provoke an exchange of hits on the bar-point. For example White may roll 42, played 13/7* and then Black could roll 62, played bar/23, 24/18*. This exchange of hits favours Black as he gains in the race by sending one of White's checkers from his mid-point all the way back to the start. In contrast Black has only lost a few pips because it was one of his back checkers which got sent to the bar.

The second part of the move, the three, played 13/10, provides a builder for Black's home board and gives Black some flexibility on his next turn (if he has not been sent to the bar). For example, let's say White rolls 52 and plays 13/8, 24/22 and now Black rolls 51 on his next turn. He would have the choice of making his opponent's bar-point with 24/18 or his own 5-pt with 10/5, 6/5. The correct play would be to make his 5-pt.

Playing 24/18, 13/10 quite often leads to complex games with lots of early hitting.

In contrast the second option, 24/15 as shown here:

38

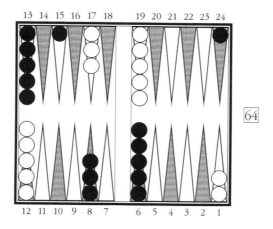

64

is an attempt to race for home. If White does not roll a number that hits the checker on his 10-pt then Black will, in all likelihood, be able to move it to safety next time. He will then have successfully escaped one of his rear checkers.

24/15 leads to much simpler games. We will see in later chapters that, particularly in tournament situations, it is sometimes right to play for complexity and sometimes for simplicity and this can quite often be determined by the choice of opening move.

Beginners facing a superior opponent should opt for 24/15 and try to keep the game simple.

62

The arguments for the split or run choice for 63 apply equally well to 62 – the two moves are very similar. So the complex option is 24/18, 13/11:

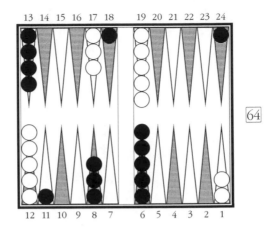

and the simpler option is 24/16 as shown below:

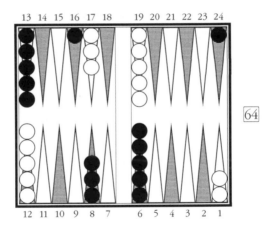

When I first started playing backgammon (1979), 62 was commonly played 13/5. However, as theory developed, the need to move the back checkers early in the game became apparent and I have seen 13/5 played only a couple of times in the last few years.

The vast majority of players move 24/18 and 13/10 or 13/11 with 63 and 62 – the pure running plays are falling into disuse as players strive for complexity, often on the (erroneous) assumption that they are stronger than their opponent!

40

If you have never read a book or had a lesson then the likelihood is that you will make the simple running plays. I know I did. When I bought my second book, "Backgammon for Profit" by Joe Dwek, I learnt the concept of splitting to my opponent's bar-point and I quickly recouped the cost of the book with my improved playing style. This is actually true of the majority of backgammon books – they may seem expensive but they very quickly pay for themselves.

In the 1970s a gentleman by the name of Bruce Becker wrote a book called "Backgammon for Blood". Becker was a very weak player but like many others at the time he wanted to cash in on the backgammon craze. He advocated playing 13/7, 13/10 with 63 and 13/7, 13/11 with 62. The idea with both of these plays is to quickly build a strong home board.

Sadly it is the wrong idea and it often leads to an exchange of hits on Black's bar-point. When this happens it is now Black who loses ground in the race when his checkers get sent back. Remember that backgammon is fundamentally a race so getting an early lead is to be encouraged.

Split or Slot Rolls

In this section we are going to look at three more rolls: 21, 41 and 51.

Each of these rolls can be played in at least two ways and we will examine the pros and cons of the various plays.

Let us remind ourselves of what we are trying to do in the opening:

- Make new points
- Mobilise the back checkers
- Unstack the heavy points

If this book were being written in the 1970s there would be little discussion. At that time most players slotted with the one, playing it 6/5. The style of that era was to slot key points and then make them next roll if possible. Very little thought was given to the risks involved and some considered that splitting the back checkers with 24/23 was riskier than slotting the 5-pt.

Time and computers have taught us a great deal and we now know that there are arguments for both approaches and that these are subtly different for the three moves.

However, there are some common themes. Slotting the 5-pt by playing 6/5 is an attempt to make your own 5-pt as quickly as possible. If your opponent does not hit the blot immediately you will be a strong favourite to make the point next turn. The game may then evolve in many different ways but quite often it will become a prime versus prime game (see Chapter 11), the most difficult of all backgammon games.

Be aware then that slotting will often lead to complex positions. Splitting, on the other hand, often leads to much simpler positions, most typically mutual holding games or high anchor positions (these game types will also be discussed in Chapter 11).

This leads us once again to the question of evaluating your strength against that of your opponent and how to adjust your play based on that evaluation. If you are the stronger player you should seek both complexity and long games and so you should be inclined to slot. The more complex the position the more chance there will be for your weaker opponent to go wrong – the longer the game the more chance you will have to utilise your skill advantage.

Conversely if you are the weaker player you should avoid complexity and instead steer for simple positions. This would indicate splitting rather than slotting.

Firstly let's discount the beginner's move 13/10. Whilst not unreasonable, it is not as productive as the other two moves that we shall discuss. The opening is the time when we can take risks to strengthen our position and whilst 13/10 unstacks a heavy point and prepares to make new points it is not as dynamic as the other two moves, both of which do two good things.

The first move to consider is 13/11, 6/5, shown here:

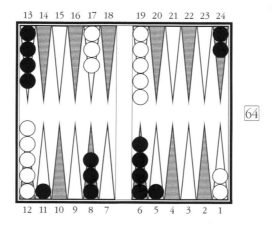

This unstacks the two heaviest points and slots the most important point on the board - your own 5-pt. If White does not hit this blot (and he is not favourite to do so) then Black is an overwhelming favourite to make the point on his next turn.

If White does hit the blot then the Black blot on the 11-pt is well placed to return hit on the 5-pt next turn. This is because it is six points away from the blot and a 6 is the one number Black cannot use to re-enter.

The alternative play is the split, 13/11, 24/23:

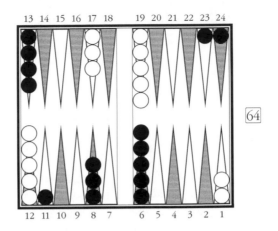

The objective of the split is twofold. It makes it more dangerous for White to bring builders into his outer board and it gives Black several good rolls next turn to make an advanced anchor (a strong defensive point in your opponent's board). For example 32 can be played 24/21, 23/21.

The split is less risky than the slot and consequently the rewards are not as high. When the slot works you will own your 5-pt, a significant improvement. When the split shows a profit it is normally by way of an advanced anchor or a hit in White's outer board. These are gains not to be ignored but the 5-pt asset is the biggest gain you can make in the opening.

For this reason the computer programs all recommend slotting as the best play and it is what I also recommend to my pupils.

41

So do we just apply the same arguments to 41 and come up with the same conclusions? Sadly backgammon is not that simple and we must look more deeply.

Again we shall first discount the beginner's move 13/8 for much the same reasons we discarded 13/10 as a viable alternative for our 21 opening. Whilst it is completely safe and brings another useful builder to Black's 8-pt it just does not do enough at a time when you should be taking risks to improve your position.

Now let's looks at the other two moves:

Firstly the slot, 13/9, 6/5:

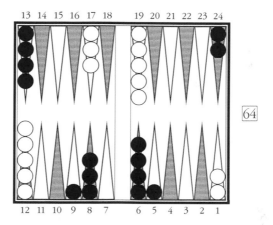

and secondly the split, 13/9, 24/23:

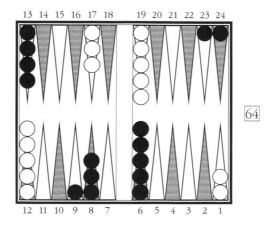

The general theories of slot vs. split apply to these moves just as they do to our 21 opener. However, there are some mathematical differences that make this a much closer call:

- After the slot, White has more numbers that will hit one of Black's blots.
- Because Black's builder is on the 9-pt rather than the 11-pt he has more point making rolls next turn even without slotting. Therefore slotting with the 1 may be taking too much extra risk for insufficient additional gain.
- If the slotted blot is hit then Black no longer has a builder the optimal six points away (remember 6 is the one number Black cannot use to enter from the bar) and the checker on the 9-pt is less effective for hitting back.

These may seem like small differences but small differences are what backgammon is all about. The computers would have us believe that these differences are enough to make the split 13/9, 24/23 the correct play with an opening 41.

I think they are probably right but that does not take into account the opponent factor. Against a weak opponent I will always play 13/9, 6/5 seeking the complexity that I believe gives me the edge. Against an opponent of equal strength or a stronger opponent I will elect for 13/9, 24/23.

One final point with regard to 41. There are some other alternatives such as 24/20, 24/23 and 24/20, 6/5. Over time these moves have been removed from the list of serious contenders. The former does not take the option of unstacking the overloaded mid-point. The latter is just too bold. Splitting the back checkers and slotting in your home board in the same move is rarely correct.

51

And so what about 51? Again there are subtle differences. Let us look at the two moves, comparing the slot, 13/8, 6/5:

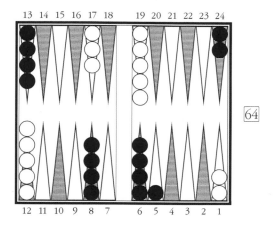

with the split, 13/8, 24/23:

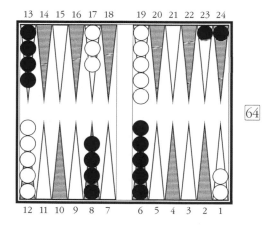

The problem with both moves is that the '5' does not really improve Black's position. He already has builders on his 8-pt. Another checker there is only a marginal improvement. However, most 5's play poorly in the opening and we have to play what the dice gods give us. 13/8 is really the only option.

The problem with the slot is that when White misses the shot at the blot, Black is only two-thirds favourite to make his 5-pt rather than being the very strong favourite after the 21 and 41 slot plays.

47

For this reason the computers again prefer the split play 13/8, 24/23, although it is close. As with the 41 play I always play the slot against weaker opponents and in this instance also against equal opponents. Only against a much stronger opponent do I play the split.

With 51 there is a third alternative that gained some popularity a few years ago but it is not often seen nowadays. I think, however, that it is worth considering. The move is 24/18.

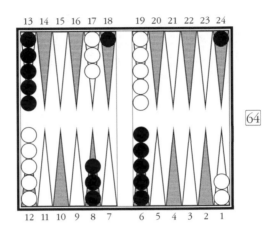

The theory behind this play is similar to that for the 63 and 62 moves that we have already considered. It seeks to enable Black either to make White's bar-point next turn or to promote an advantageous (to Black) sequence of hits on White's bar-point. It also uses the 5 effectively which neither the slotting nor the splitting play does.

I think this move should be tried from time to time, not only for the shock factor, but because it is a genuine contender.

The best way forward for any individual is to try each of these moves, see what type of game develops from each, and learn what you are comfortable with. Never forget that you are playing another human being - this may well be the determining factor.

Rolls with No Broad Agreement

52

52 is a poor opening roll. Firstly let's rule out the beginner's move 13/6. It is safe but this move does nothing to improve Black's position and does not follow the objectives we have set ourselves.

With 52 there are only two sensible alternatives. The first move to consider is 13/8, 13/11, shown here:

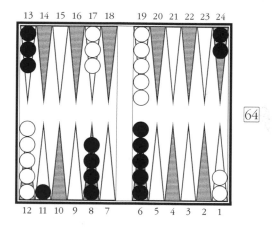

This unstacks the mid-point and brings a builder into play on the 11-pt. A builder on the 11-pt is not as useful as one on the 10-pt or 9-pt as it only bears directly on the 5-pt in the home board. On the plus side it can only be hit by White with a 64.

The alternative is to split the back checkers with 13/8, 24/22:

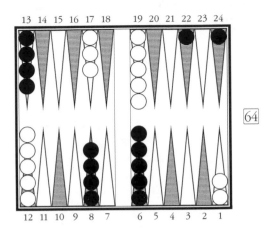

For years nobody played this move because they feared being wiped out by 55 or 33 from White. However, these are only two of the possible 36 rolls and for many of White's other rolls the split works well by deterring him from freely placing builders in his outer board.

As with other moves we have examined, the building play 13/8, 13/11 tends to produce more complex positions than 13/8, 24/22. The latter play often leads to mutual holding games (see Chapter 11).

The computers show a slight preference for 13/8, 24/22 but it is really a matter of personal preference.

54

With 54 there are three options. The first of these is now virtually never seen and that is the old-fashioned running play 24/15. It is not so much that this is a terrible play but rather that the other two plays are that much better. So let us look at the alternatives. Firstly, the building play 13/8, 13/9:

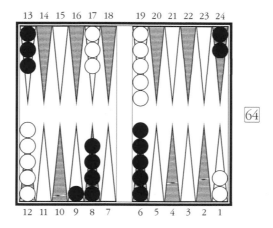

As with other building plays the theme here is to bring builders into position to make new home board points. Stacking another builder on the 8-pt is not ideal but you can only play what the dice give you. If left alone Black has good numbers such as 41, 52, 43 etc. to make new points next time. The other alternative is to play the 5 the same way and slot your opponent's 5-pt with the 4 by playing 13/8, 24/20:

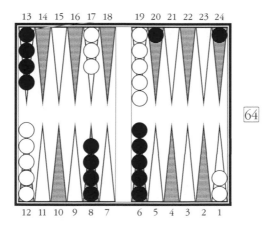

This is a bold attempt to fight for your opponent's 5-pt. White should hit the blot with most 1's and 3's, leaving his own blot if necessary. Such is the importance of the two 5-pts in the early game that both sides should take risks to establish them. For example, if White rolls

53 in response to the splitting play then his correct move is 13/5* and not 8/3, 6/3.

When the splitting play succeeds it normally gains more than the building play and perhaps this is why computers prefer splitting. However it is a marginal choice and you should play the move with which you are most comfortable.

64

The arguments for two of the plays with 64 are more or less identical to the discussion we had earlier when we covered the 63 and 62 opening rolls. The simplest play is to run with 24/14:

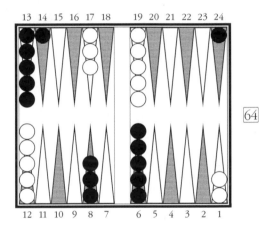

The argument for running with 64 is slightly stronger than that for 63 and 62. Black leaves only 11 hitting numbers and the blot, if not hit, can be moved to relative safety more easily next turn than is the case with 62 and 63.

One of the arguments against running that applies to 62, 63 and 64 is that next turn, if the blot is missed, Black will have to take the time to move it to safety.

The alternative is the split play 24/18, 13/9:

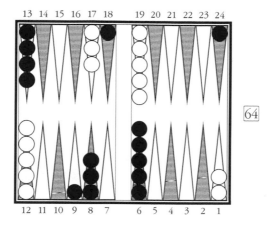

As with 63 and 62 this can lead to very complex games with lots of early hits and counter-hits. If you are the better player then this play is preferable to the running 64, which usually leads to relatively straightforward positions.

64 provides us with a third option, namely making the 2-pt with 8/2, 6/2:

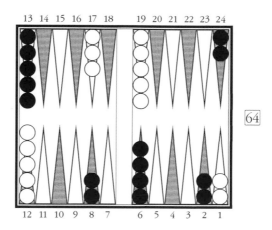

Can it be wrong to make a home board point? The answer is maybe. Conventional wisdom says that the point made is too deep in the home board so early in the game. Conventional wisdom also says that the 8-pt and the 2-pt cannot both be points in the same prime so why make the 2-pt when you already have the 8-pt?

A hundred years ago this would have been a popular play. Thirty years ago you would have been laughed at for making this play. When the first version of JellyFish, the first neural net backgammon program, hit the market it made the 2-pt with 64 and several top players followed suit. Then along came Snowie and the early versions said run with 24/14. The later versions gave the vote to 24/18, 13/9. eXtreme Gammon likes all three plays with a tiny preference for 24/18, 13/9.

Which is the 'best' play? Nobody really knows and yet again it is down to personal preference and the type of game with which you are comfortable. Occasionally playing 8/2, 6/2 is no bad thing because many players do not know the correct responses to what is a relatively unusual play.

43

There are four reasonable ways to play 43. I have eliminated the 'safe' 13/6 which does nothing whatsoever to improve Black's position. There are three splitting plays available, the first of which is probably the most common. This is 24/20, 13/10 shown below:

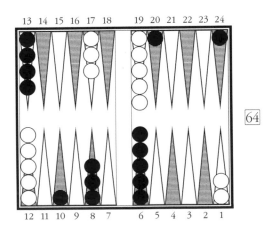

This move plays well to our basic criteria. It slots the point in your opponent's board that you would most like to make (his 5-pt), whilst unstacking your mid-point by bringing down a builder to your own 10-pt.

In response White should hit the blot on his 5-pt if he can (there are a few exceptions, for example with 61 he would play 13/7, 8/7) and then a battle for that point will ensue.

The first splitting alternative is to vary the split slightly by going to the 21-pt (your opponent's 4-pt) by playing 24/21, 13/9:

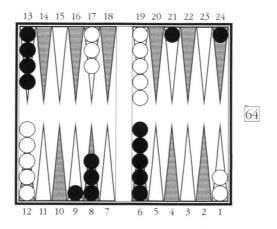

The fact that you have slotted the slightly less useful 21-pt is compensated by the fact that the builder on your 9-pt is slightly more useful than the one on the 10-pt (it bears upon more home board points).

There is virtually nothing to choose between these two plays and the choice is up to you. Something worth noting is that White's correct response is often to hit loose on his 4-pt, for example with 54 he should play 13/4*.

Whilst many players know it is correct to hit loose on the 5-pt after their opponent has split there, not everyone knows that it is also correct to hit loose on the 4-pt. For this reason strong players often prefer 24/21, 13/9 to 24/20, 13/10.

The final splitting option with 43 is to split with both checkers 24/20, 24/21:

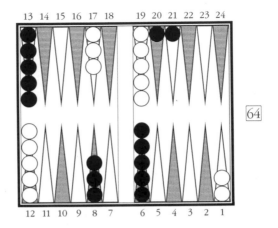

This move was popular with German players in the early 1990s but has largely fallen into disuse. However it has its merits, particularly at some match scores where you are seeking to avoid a gammon. Playing 24/20, 24/21 virtually guarantees that Black will make a high anchor and get into some sort of holding game (see Chapter 11).

Again, a weak White player may not know the correct responses to this play. For example a 21 should be played 6/5*, 6/4* hitting both checkers. I wouldn't suggest playing 24/20, 24/21 all the time but used occasionally it has its merits.

The final option with 43 is to pull two checkers off the mid-point with 13/9, 13/10:

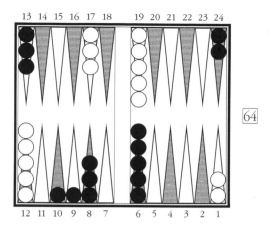

This is a bold attempt to build a prime quickly. If neither of the blots is hit, Black will make at least one new point next turn. Playing two checkers down like this often leads to prime versus prime games that are among the most complex in backgammon.

In the 1970s two checkers down was the standard play and then in the 1980s and 1990s 24/20, 13/10 and 24/21, 13/9 were the preferred plays. Once the neural net programs started to have their say, 13/9, 13/10 came back into fashion and the current versions of Snowie, gnubg and XG all rate this play as best.

I maintain a database of the opening rolls from some 15,000 games (and growing) and my own analysis also shows 13/9, 13/10 as the best choice for 43.

32

Virtually everything that we have said about 43 also applies to 32. Thus we can rule out 13/8 as adding no value and we are left with the choice of two splits or bringing two builders down.

The first of the splits is 24/21, 13/11:

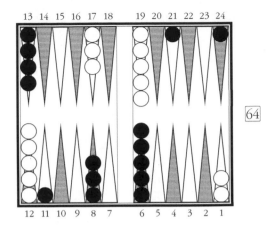

This fulfils our basic criteria and balances advancing a back checker with bringing down a new builder. White's correct response, as noted above, is often to hit loose on his 4-pt.

The second split is 24/22, 13/10:

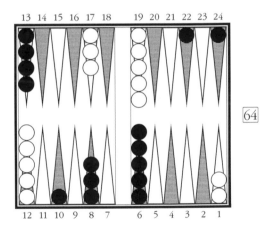

Unlike 43 where the two splits are virtually equal this split for 32 is weaker than the alternative. It slots a less valuable point and also leaves Black vulnerable to both 33 and 55 in response by White. Because of this it is rarely seen nowadays.

The real alternative to 24/21, 13/11 is the building play 13/10, 13/11:

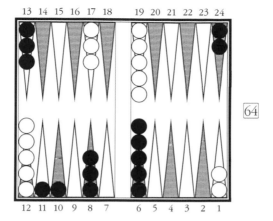

As with the equivalent play with 43 this is an attempt to build new points quickly and will often lead to a prime versus prime type of game.

Once more this was the standard play in the 1970s and then the splitting plays became fashionable in the 1980s and 1990s. The difference, however, is that once the computers came along they supported the splitting play 24/21, 13/11 over the two checkers down option.

In certain match situations (discussed later) then two down is clearly correct. In money play the moves are close enough that the choice is purely one of personal style but note that the computers still have a slight preference for the split 24/21, 13/11.

Summary

So, as we can see, there are different ways to play the opening rolls in many cases and the choice is really up to you. You need to be comfortable with the moves that you make and you will quickly learn what types of positions evolve from each of the various choices.

If you are a beginner I recommend trying out some of the alternative plays until you find the ones that suit your playing style.

Opening theory is constantly evolving and computers will no doubt throw further light on this area in future but the information in this chapter will provide you with more than enough to be going on with.

In the next chapter we will look briefly at the responses to the opening rolls.

Chapter 6:   Responses to the Opening Rolls

Basic Strategy

In the preceding chapter we looked at how to play the 15 opening rolls and saw that there are approximately 30 reasonable ways to play those rolls.

On the first response we have the possibility of throwing 21 different numbers – 15 non-doubles and the six doubles. This gives us about 600 different positions that we can reach after only one move each by the two players. Looking at all 600 positions is obviously way beyond the scope of this book – indeed they would merit a book on their own.

The objective of this chapter is to set out some general principles that you can use when responding to the opening roll. As we shall see in a later chapter, computers have had a huge influence on backgammon and one of the results is that opening theory has evolved considerably during this century. You might think that after 5,000 years we might have worked out how to reply to the opening move but that is not the case and one of the fascinations of the game is that it is still evolving.

The first few moves of any game are critical as they will determine the course of play for many moves to come.

In general the objectives when responding are very similar to those for the opening roll – you should try to make new points, activate the back checkers and unstack the mid-point and the 6-pt.

However, we can add at least two more:

- If your opponent has slotted a point, hitting that slot (if possible) should be a priority.

- If you can hit one of his builders in the outer board you should probably do so.

One thing you can do when responding that you can't do on the opening roll is to roll a double and quite often this will give you an early advantage. I will now look at some of the common themes when responding to an opening roll.

Destroying a slot

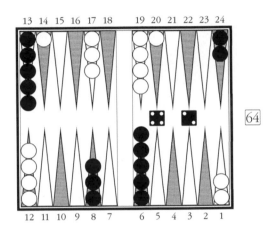

White has rolled 21 and played the slotting play 13/11, 6/5. Black now rolls 42. How would you play it?

If you follow the basic objectives you will make your own 4-pt with 8/4, 6/4. But look ahead. In all probability White will make his own 5-pt next turn and will then have the better position because his development will be superior. A much better play is 24/20*, 13/11 sending the blot to the bar. This play has three very positive effects:

- It sends White's checker to the bar.

- It slots White's 5-pt.

- Black takes the lead in the race.

62

Backgammon involves balancing risks and rewards. Here the rewards are high and the risks minimal (although you do not get the benefit of making your own 4-pt) so 24/20*, 13/11 is the standout play.

Here's a second example:

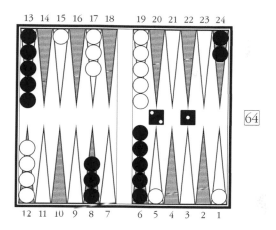

White has opened with 43, played 13/10, 24/20. How should you play 21 as Black?

You could avoid the battle and quietly play 24/21 but battles (in the main) aren't won by staying in the trenches. You must fight for your 5-pt and play 13/11, 6/5*. A war may then be fought over your 5-pt. Sometimes you will be victorious and at other times your opponent will triumph, but that is the very nature of the game.

Playing passively in the opening is likely to leave you with the inferior position.

One of backgammon's oldest adages is: "When in doubt, hit" and in the opening hitting will often leave you with the advantage. The next example looks at balancing hitting against point-building.

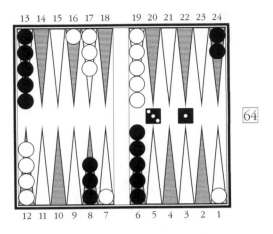

White has played his 64 by moving 24/18, 13/9. Black responds with 31. Would you hit with 8/7* with the 1 and play either 13/10 or 24/21 with the 3?

If you did you would be making a small error. The 5-pt is so important that Black should pass up the hit in favour of making his 5-pt with 8/5, 6/5.

To show you that backgammon can sometimes be a game of fine detail let's consider what you as Black should do if you had rolled 42 instead of 31 – would you make your 4-pt or hit?

Did you make your 4-pt? If you did you would be making a tiny error. Because the 4-pt is not as strong as the 5-pt it turns out that hitting is slightly the better play. This just shows how tricky backgammon can be.

Gaining a Tempo

In the opening, taking away your opponent's freedom to choose how to play half his roll next turn by hitting a blot can gain you a very useful tempo. Let's give White the same opening roll of 64 played 24/18, 13/9 and ask how Black should play 54 as his responding roll. The position is shown here:

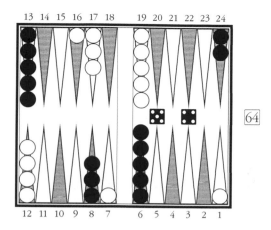

However Black plays his 54 he will be leaving a blot for White to shoot at somewhere on the board. If that is the case then why not restrict White's options on his next roll by hitting his blot? It may look odd, at least at first, but the correct play is 6/1*, 24/20.

This move slots a point Black would love to make - his opponent's 5-pt – and, as noted before, ensures that White must use half of his next roll (excepting doubles) to enter from the bar. That will make it impossible for him to make a new home board point on his next roll unless he rolls a double.

Playing 13/8, 24/20 is not as good because it gives White his full roll to play next turn and you can be sure he will attack Black's blot on his 5-pt if he possibly can.

You will notice that after the hitting play most of White's rolls containing a 6 play poorly next turn – especially 66.

Suppose White has opened with 32 and played 24/21, 13/11. How should Black play 54? The answer, which may surprise you, is 13/4*. Again, the tempo play is far better than any other.

Changing Priorities

While you have a free choice with some of your opening rolls, when it comes to your first response you must take your opponent's opening move into account.

Consider this position where White has opened with a 53 making his 3-pt.

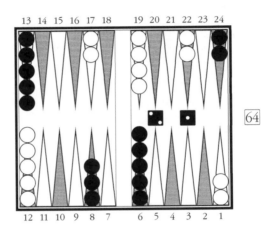

As Black you now roll 21. Are splitting and slotting still of equal merit?

The answer is no. Slotting is now too dangerous as White has a second home board point which will limit Black's re-entry from the bar if he is hit. Now the splitting play becomes mandatory and Black must play 13/11, 24/23. An advantage of the splitting play is that White cannot use one of the checkers on his 8-pt to make a new home board point without exposing the other checker to a direct shot. For example, with a 31 he will make his 5-pt but there will be a blot on his 8-pt.

Here are some guiding principles to use when replying to the opening move:

- Once your opponent has used his spare checker (in the opening position) on his 8-pt to make a new home board point it is normally correct to split your back checkers in response (see example above).

- If your opponent splits to your 5-pt with his opening move and you roll a hitting number such as 41 you should hit with the 1 (6/5*) and then play the other half of the roll by moving off your mid-point.

- If your opponent splits to your bar-point with his opening move and you roll a hitting number such as 62 you should hit with the 6 and then play the other half of the roll by splitting your back checkers. If you roll 65 you should play 13/7*, 6/1* putting two White checkers on the bar.

- If your opponent makes a new home board point with his opening roll and you can't make one of your own you should try to split the rear checkers. This applies even to rolls containing a 6 such as 62. Here is an example:

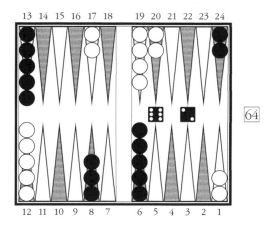

White has opened with 31 making his 5-pt. When Black rolls 62 in response his best move is 24/18, 13/11. This might look risky but it is an attempt to equalise the position as soon as possible. It may not work but the opening is the time to take risks and that is the case here.

In the last few years computers have made us change our minds about several of the first responses. Here is an example:

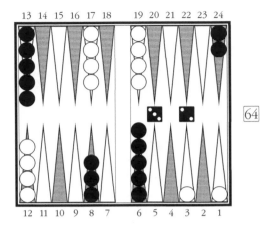

White has opened with 52 and played 13/8, 24/22. Black responds with 32.

For many years it was thought that the best play was 6/3*/1* putting both White checkers on the bar. Recent analysis, however, has shown that the best move, albeit by a whisker, is 13/11, 6/3*.

The double hit leaves a poor structure while 13/11, 6/3* unstacks the two points that start with the most checkers and that development slightly outweighs the advantages of the double hit.

The only time that a reply to the opening move should be used to hit two checkers in your home board with a non-double is when your opponent opens with 21, 41 or 51 and plays 24/23 with the 1. If you then roll 41 the correct play is 6/2*/1*.

Playing Doubles

On your opening roll you can't roll a double. That is not true of the first response when rolling a double will normally give you the advantage. One piece of advice is that you should try to do two good things rather than one when you roll a double. Here is a case in point:

68

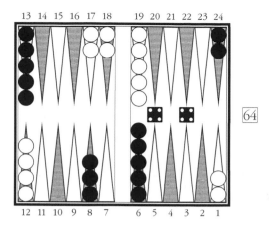

This position arises after White opens with a 61 and makes his bar-point. How should Black play double 4?

Black could run his two rear checkers all the way to the 16-pt by playing 24/16(2). Alternatively he could make his own 5-pt by playing 13/5(2). Both these moves do one good thing but Black can do much better.

With the first two 4's he should play 24/20(2), taking possession of his opponent's 5-pt. With the other two 4's he should play 13/9(2). That unstacks the heavy mid-point and makes a new outer board point. It might seem that 8/4(2) would be a better use of those last two 4's but in fact the distribution of checkers is better after 13/9(2) and that play doesn't leave a blot on the 8-pt.

In general, when you roll a double as the first response, you should move two pairs of checkers and make new points. This is normally much better than hitting. Here is an example:

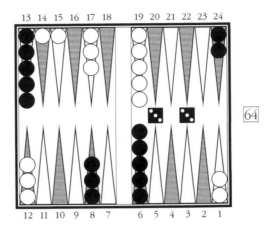

White has played 13/10, 13/11 with an opening 32. Black has responded with double 3. He could hit with 24/15* and then play 24/21 with the remaining 3.

However, Black will have a much stronger position after playing 24/21(2), 8/5(2) which gives him his own 5-pt and his opponent's 4-pt. These two long-term assets far outweigh the temporary gain from hitting. 8/5(2), 6/3(2), making two home board points is also very reasonable.

The one exception to this rule is when your opponent slots his 5-pt on his opening turn with 41 by playing 13/9, 6/5. If you now roll double 1 then you should hit with 24/20*. However, to demonstrate that backgammon is far from trivial, if your opponent slots his 5-pt with 21 (13/11, 6/5) or 51 (13/8, 6/5) and you roll 11 in response then the correct play is 8/7(2), 6/5(2).

As noted in the introduction to this chapter I cannot cover all the first responses to the opening move. If I provided a list of all the correct responses you would in all likelihood quickly forget them. However, if you apply the general principles laid out in this chapter they will set you on the road to winning backgammon.

Chapter 7: A Little Arithmetic and Basic Tactics

Skills

To become a good backgammon player there are three fundamental areas of skill and knowledge that you need to understand and gradually master: pattern recognition, psychology and arithmetic.

Pattern Recognition

Above all else backgammon is a game of pattern recognition. Because of the number of possible moves at any one turn, the number of possible positions in a game is very large. There are 36 possible rolls of two dice. Ignoring for the moment that some rolls are duplicated (e.g. 21 and 12), after two rolls by you and two by your opponent we already have 36x36x36x36 = 1,679,616 possible combinations. Given that each roll could be played up to 20 different ways, you begin to get some idea of the numbers involved.

We cannot therefore learn hundreds (or even thousands) of specific positions in the same way that a chess player does. What we have to recognise is that whilst specific positions do not often repeat themselves - except some opening sequences and endings - certain types of position constantly repeat. As we will see in Chapter 11, most backgammon games follow a number of common themes. It is vital to understand the basic strategies for each type of position and then to apply those basics to the position in front of you in a specific game.

You can only do that if you have a 'mental store' of similar positions that you have seen or read about before. All good players have a comprehensive store of reference positions for each game type which they constantly use in their decision-making processes. Over time you will build up your own library of reference positions and use them in your own games.

These positions will form part of what I call your 'Backgammon Model'. When you first learn to play you effectively begin with a blank sheet. On this sheet you first load the rules of the game and your initial playing style. Over time and through experience you build up your library of reference positions and refine your playing style. This is a constant process that continues throughout your backgammon life. How good you become is largely determined by the quality of information in your model and, crucially, how you apply it to real-life play.

Psychology

Never forget that you are playing another human being. When you play against a computer it consistently makes the correct logical decision in any given position. Human beings do not.

You have to learn how to analyse your opponent's playing style and get to understand his strengths and weaknesses. You can then use these to your advantage in over-the-board play. As a simple example, we have already seen that certain ways of playing an opening roll can lead to complex positions whilst a different choice for the same roll might lead to a much simpler type of game. If your opponent does not like complex positions the choice of how to play the opening roll has just been made for you.

Human beings are particularly vulnerable when it comes to the doubling cube and all the emotion that can surround it. The biggest errors in any game nearly always involve the doubling cube. We will look at this particular aspect of psychology in some examples later.

Naturally if you are playing a complete unknown this is more difficult but a lot of the time you will be playing against people you know well or have at least heard about. You can improve your win rate considerably by taking the time to study your opponents.

A detailed study of games psychology as applied to backgammon is beyond the scope of this book but if you are interested in this topic see the bibliography for further suggested reading.

Arithmetic

Backgammon is played with dice. As we have already seen, how well you play will depend upon a number of things but you must have a grasp of the basic arithmetic of the game.

At the very least you need to be able to count shots, work out who is winning the race and have a grasp of elementary probability (as it applies to the game). We will cover these topics in the second half of this chapter.

To succeed at the highest levels normally means becoming successful at tournament play – although there are some very successful pure money players. To become really good at tournament play you need to understand, and be able to use, match equity tables. A match equity table is something that gives you your percentage winning chances from any score in a match. For example, leading 5-4 in a match to 7 points your match winning chances are about 60%. I will touch on this briefly in the chapter on tournament play and also point you towards more detailed material on the topic.

Other Skills

There are other skills necessary to become a top-flight backgammon player. In the main these skills are common to many successful games players and sportsmen. They are: concentration, self-control, self-confidence and physical fitness.

This latter might seem surprising but it is no good playing well for seven hours and then losing heavily in the final hour of the session because you cannot concentrate (note the linkage between the skills). Needless to say, drinking any form of alcohol when playing backgammon (other than a social game for trivial stakes) is not a good idea!

A Little Arithmetic

Number Theory

Firstly let us look at the rolls of the dice. When you roll two dice with the numbers 1 to 6 on each face, there are 36 possible combinations, as we saw in Chapter 5.

As a reminder there are 15 different number combinations that can each occur two ways. For example, 12 can be thrown as a "1" on the first die and a "2" on the second, or a "2" on the first die and a "1" on the second. (If you have a problem visualising this then perform the experiment with two different coloured dice.) In contrast the six doubles can be thrown only one way and therefore throwing a particular double is only half as likely as throwing a particular non-double. You cannot start the game with a double so, as we have already seen, there are only 15 possible opening rolls – there being no difference between 12 and 21.

In backgammon you often need to know how many rolls contain a specific number. For example, how many of the 36 rolls contain a 1? The answer is eleven. The way to arrive at this figure is to suppose that the first die lands on a 1. Whatever the second die lands on we have six rolls that contain a 1: 11, 12, 13, 14, 15 and 16. The same is true if the second die lands on 1, then we have: 11, 21, 31, 41, 51 and 61 giving twelve in all. But notice we have counted 11 twice so we must subtract one from twelve to give the answer eleven.

What about if you need to roll one of two numbers, say a 4 or a 5? Then, without showing the arithmetic, I will tell you that the answer is that 20 of the 36 rolls contain a 4 or a 5. If you need one of three numbers the answer is 27, four numbers is 32 and five numbers is 35.

This is not the whole story as numbers can also be thrown using a combination of the two dice. For example, a six could be thrown by rolling 42. In fact six is the easiest number to roll in backgammon. There are 17 ways to roll a 6:

- All natural 6's (eleven)
- 42 and 24 (two)
- 51 and 15 (two)
- 22 (one)
- 33(one)

For the other numbers up to six the table looks like this:

- 1 - all natural 1's (eleven)
- 2 - all natural 2's plus 11 (twelve)
- 3 - all natural 3's plus, 21, 12 and 11 (fourteen)
- 4 - all natural 4's plus 31, 13, 11 and 22 (fifteen)
- 5 - all natural 5's plus 32, 23, 41 and 14 (fifteen)

What about numbers greater than 6 where a combination is always required?

- 7 – six rolls (61, 16, 52, 25, 43, 34)
- 8 – six rolls (62, 26, 53, 35, 22, 44)
- 9 – five rolls (63, 36, 54, 45, 33)
- 10 – three rolls (64, 46, 55)
- 11 – two rolls 65, 56)
- 12 – three rolls (33, 44, 66)
- 15 – one roll (55)
- 16 – one roll (44)
- 18 - one roll (66)
- 20 – one roll (55)
- 24 – one roll (66)

As a point of information the average of all 36 dice rolls is 8.1667. We shall use this fact later in the book.

Having established these basic facts we need to see how to apply them in real life. First let us consider the case where, despite our best efforts, we have to leave a blot for our opponent to aim at. How far away from our opponent's potential hitter should we leave it?

We have seen that within a distance of six pips or fewer our opponent will have at least 11 numbers that hit and that if we must leave a blot within 6 pips it should be as close to our opponent as possible.

For distances of 7 and 8 pips the number of hitting rolls is identical and thereafter the chances of getting hit diminish as the distance gets greater (with the exception of exactly 12 pips). Therefore if we do not have to come within direct range (i.e. six or fewer pips) we should stay further away if we can – although there may be other factors to take into account. Here's a simple example:

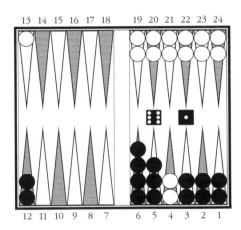

In this position Black has a 61 to play. With the 6 he will bring one checker home with 12/6. With the 1 he can then play either 12/11 or 6/5. Is there any difference? The answer is yes (it nearly always is in backgammon).

If he moves 12/11 he will be vulnerable to 6 shots – any seven. If instead he plays 6/5 then he will be hit by only five shots. This is because White will not be able to hit with 22 as Black owns the 6-pt. One extra shot may not seem like much but look at it from White's perspective – he increases his hitting numbers from 5 to 6, a whopping 20% improvement.

An early game example shows how we can use our number theory very simply:

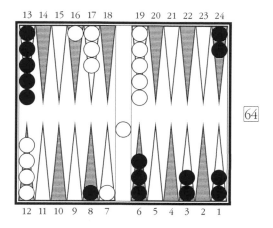

This position occurs after White opens with 64: 24/18, 13/9 and Black responds with 55: 8/3(2), 6/1(2)*. The first question is how often will White fail to enter his checker from the bar next turn?

To enter, White's next roll must contain a 2, 4 or 5. We have seen that his chance of rolling one of three specific numbers is 27 in 36 (i.e. 27 of the 36 rolls allow him to enter). The other nine times - when he rolls, 61, 16, 63, 36, 31, 13, 66, 33 or 11 - he must stay on the bar. Therefore he has a 75% chance of entering.

If he stays on the bar then how often will Black hit one of the other two White blots that are exposed? Consider the one on Black's bar-point first. Black will hit with any natural 1 or 6 (20 numbers). He will also hit with 42, 24, 22 and 33 (4 numbers), giving us 24 hits so far.

What about the blot on White's 9-pt? Black can hit with 62, 26, 53, 35, 44 and 22 (six numbers). However we have already counted, 62, 26 and 22 so we cannot count them again. That leaves three new numbers and so our overall chance of hitting one of the two blots is 27 numbers – again 75%.

I hope this gives you some idea of the application of number theory. We will now extend our thinking to add a few more ideas.

Basic Tactics

Move Selection

Every time it is your turn to play you roll the dice. Having done that you have to choose the best play. Sometimes this is easy but most of the time you have quite a lot of choices. First here is a simple principle:

- You must decide which moves are possible – we call these candidate plays – and then select which candidate move gives you the best chance of winning.

As a simple demonstration look at this position with Black to play 32:

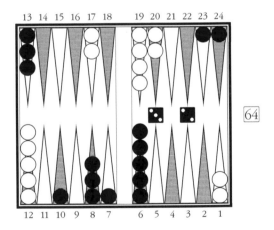

An inexperienced beginner looking at this position will see that he can cover the blot on his bar point and will quickly play the 3 by moving 10/7. He will then look around for a suitable 2 and will play 24/22, 13/11, 23/21 or even 8/6.

He may never consider 7/4, 6/4 or 8/5, 7/5 or 24/21, 23/21 as candidate plays, despite the fact each of them is very much better than any move that makes the bar-point. The best play is actually 8/5, 7/5.

There are a couple of key themes to take away from this:

- Make sure you have considered all the candidate plays. Spending time choosing between Play A and Play B is fine but if the best move is Play C you will have missed a trick.

- Never take any part of your move unless it is truly forced, for example, entering a checker from the bar when there is only one point on which it can enter, before considering the move as a whole. The rules of backgammon allow you to try out as many moves as you like before lifting the dice. If you are unsure of which move to play, try them all before making a decision. Quite often seeing the resulting positions will help the decision making process.

Hitting

We have already seen that when you are hit you must re-enter from the bar in order to continue to play and that you will need to use half of your next roll, that is one of the two dice, to do so.

It should be obvious that putting two opposing checkers on the bar is a huge advantage. Your opponent will have to use all of his next roll to re-enter those checkers (unless he rolls a lucky double) and quite often he will be able to enter only one of the two checkers.

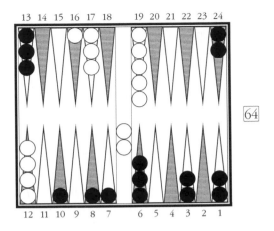

Continuing the game from the second position in this chapter, let us assume White failed to enter by rolling 61 and then Black followed with 63 and played 13/7*, 13/10. Now White has two checkers on the bar and is in dire trouble. On his next turn he will still have both checkers on the bar 25% of the time and there is only a 25% chance that he will he be able to enter both checkers. The remaining 50% of the time he will enter one checker and have one remaining on the bar.

Thus we can see that hitting is powerful and hitting two or more checkers even more powerful. As I have mentioned before, 'when in doubt, hit'.

Tactical Hitting

When you hit you have to consider the possibility of being hit back. However, in the opening it is so important to fight for control of the key points on the board (particularly the two 5-pts) that, even when you are likely to be hit back, hitting is the right play.

Look at the position after White opens with 54 played 13/8, 24/20 and Black rolls a 21 in response:

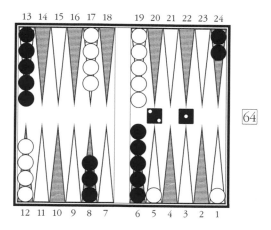

The correct play of the 21 is 13/11, 6/5* putting White on the bar. Despite the fact that White has 21 return hits (all 5's and 4's – except 64 – plus 32, 23 and 22) it is still correct to hit.

This re-emphasises the point that backgammon strategy comprises balancing risk and reward. With his hitting play Black takes a substantial risk in order to achieve a strategic objective. If not hit in return he hopes to cover the blot on his 5-pt thus making that crucial point.

The other type of tactical hitting is what is called 'hit and split'. We hit with half the roll and then advance one of our back checkers with the other half. The advanced checker is protected by the fact that the opponent will need to enter with half of his roll next turn. Here is an example. White has started with 63 played 24/15 and Black has a 43 to play:

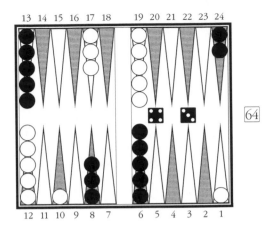

Black should hit with the 3 playing 13/10*. With the 4 he should advance 24/20. This follows our opening theory of getting the back checkers moving. In this instance he slots a point he would really like to make, his opponent's 5-pt, and does so with relative impunity because White must re-enter from the bar. Note that if White should now roll 53 he should play bar/20, 8/5* continuing the fight for his 5-pt. The opening can become a real slugfest with both sides hitting for several rolls.

Making Points

Ideally when we make new points we want to do one of three things:

    1)   Make new home board points, preferably starting with the 5-pt or 4-pt. Home board points help to prevent your opponent entering.

    2)   Make points next to each other so that they form part of a prime. This is why making the 5-pt is so powerful. Not only is it a home board point, it also forms part of a potential prime with the 6-pt and the 8-pt. All you need to add is the bar-pt and, lo and behold, you have a four-point prime.

3) Make a point in your opponent's home board or his bar-pt. A point in your opponent's home board is known as an anchor. Anchors are very powerful because they protect you from attack and provide a re-entry point for any of your blots that might get hit.

Here is an example:

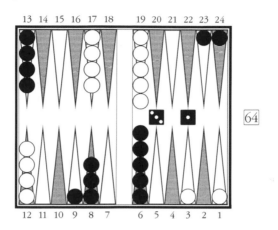

How should Black play this 31? He could play 13/10/9, making the 9-pt and leaving no blots. Alternatively he could make his 5-pt with 8/5, 6/5 but leave the blot on his 9-pt exposed to all natural 6's plus 53, 51 and 42.

The correct play is to make the 5-pt. The 5-pt is so important that Black should not pass up this opportunity despite the blot that is left. This is a simple but powerful example of how we learn to balance risk with reward. Black trades the risk of being hit next turn against the reward of making a long term asset – this is a common theme in backgammon.

Diversification and Duplication

If you have studied the basics of backgammon number theory, one thing which should be apparent is that when it is your turn you want as many of the 36 rolls as possible to be good for you. Conversely when it is your opponent's turn you want to limit his good rolls.

A very simple example of the latter is that if we own five of our six home board points and our opponent has a checker on the bar then he has only 11 good rolls - those that contain the number corresponding to the open point.

There are two general principles that we can apply to help us – diversification and duplication.

Diversification

When you watch a good backgammon player his game always seems to flow and he rarely seems to be stuck for a play in any given situation. One reason for his apparent superiority is his application of diversification. With diversification we seek to ensure that on our next move as many rolls of the dice as possible will enable us to do something constructive.

Here is an example:

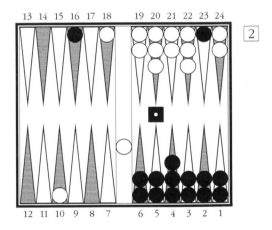

Black has to play a 1. With White closed out on the bar (that is, he cannot re-enter because Black owns all six home board points), Black has the luxury of not having to worry about White's next roll and all he need concern himself with is optimising his chances for a gammon.

He could play 16/15, but this would leave him needing a 5 to hit the checker on the 18-pt and also a 5 to hit the checker on the 10-pt. With this play he will hit with 15 of the 36 possible rolls next turn. If instead he plays 4/3 then he will still need a 5 to hit the checker on the 18-pt but will need a 6 to hit on the 10 point. This play gives him 24 hitting rolls next turn - a 60% increase.

This is a simple application of the principle of diversification. Normally one has to consider the implications of White's roll as well, but the concept occurs frequently and is one that must be learnt and practised.

Consider the opening roll of 21. Suppose that Black plays 13/11, 6/5. If the slotted checker on the 5-pt is hit, the checker on the 11 point is a hitter 6 pips away and six is the one number that Black cannot use to re-enter White's board. This is another straightforward but effective use of the principle of diversification.

Duplication

Duplication is the opposite of diversification. Here we try to make sure that we limit our opponent's constructive rolls. We do this by 'duplicating' his good numbers. For example we may leave a position where he can use a 5 to hit a blot or a 5 to make a point by covering a blot. If he then rolls a 5 he may face a difficult choice. If he doesn't roll the 5 then he will not accomplish either of his objectives.

However, if we leave him a 5 to hit or a 4 to make a point his decision will be made for him once he rolls his dice. Thus we use duplication to make life more difficult for our opponent and to limit his chances to improve his position. If he happens to roll the appropriate double that both hits and makes a point we just know it's not our day!

Here is a simple example of duplication:

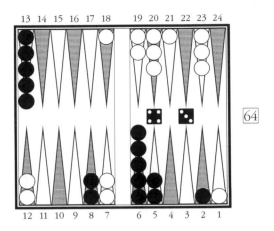

Black has to play 43. He can use the 4 to cover the blot on his 2-pt by playing 6/2. Unfortunately he cannot play the 3 safely and must leave a new blot somewhere. His sensible choices are 13/10 or 6/3.

If he plays 13/10 White will need to roll a 3 to hit the blot but notice that White also needs a 3 to play 7/4 on his own side of the board to make his 4-pt. On the other hand if Black plays 6/3 White will need a 2 to hit and still have 1's and 3's to cover the blot on his 4-pt. Playing 13/10 duplicates White's 3's and it is therefore the best play. Note also that to hit the blot on Black's 10-pt White will have to give up his anchor on Black's bar-pt (unless he rolls 63 or 33).

Chapter 8: Doubling – The Basics

Introduction

Over the last hundred years a great many books have been written on backgammon. Of this large total only four have been wholly dedicated to doubling and of those four only two are actually any good.

Why this dearth of material on what is the most difficult aspect of the game? The question provides the answer – doubling is difficult and therefore authors have shied away from it. I shall devote more space than is usual in an introductory book to the topic of doubling. However, even when I have done that I will only have grazed the surface of our knowledge and further reading will be required to develop your doubling skills,

As we saw in the brief history in Chapter 2 doubling was introduced to backgammon in the mid-1920s to spice up the game. Nobody is quite sure of the origin of doubling and there are rumours that it started in golf but I have never been able to find anything to substantiate this claim.

Doubling Basics

This is the basic theory of doubling.

Each game starts at a stake of 1 point. During the course of the game, a player who feels he (or she) has a sufficient advantage may propose doubling the stakes. The player does this by turning the doubling cube to the next higher value. Each face of the doubling cube bears a number to record progressive doubles and redoubles, starting at 2 and going on to 4, 8, 16, 32 and 64.

At the commencement of play, the doubling cube rests to one side of the board, in the centre between the two players with a displayed value of 64 (there is no 1 on the doubling cube so 64 serves as 1 at the start of the game). When it is his turn, a player who thinks he has a sufficient advantage may propose doubling the stakes, in the first instance by turning the cube to 2, and so on.

A player may double any time it is his turn and he has not yet rolled the dice. A player who is offered a double may refuse, in which case he concedes the game and pays one point. Otherwise he must accept the double and play on for the new higher stake of two points. A player who accepts a double becomes the owner of the cube, which is placed on his side of the board (showing '2'), and only he may make the next double.

Subsequent doubles in the same game are called 'redoubles'. If a player refuses a redouble he must pay the number of points that were at stake prior to the redouble. Otherwise he becomes the new owner of the cube and the game continues at twice the previous stake. There is no limit to the number of times a double may be offered in one game.

It may seem counter-intuitive to accept the doubling of the stakes when you stand worse in a game. However, consider the following two scenarios:

1) Player A doubles Player B in each of four games. Player B drops all four doubles and is therefore down four points (-4).

2) Player A doubles Player B in each of four games but this time Player B accepts the doubles. He goes on to lose three games but wins the fourth game. He loses two points in each of the games he loses (-6) and wins two points in the game he wins (+2). His net result is –4 points. The same as scenario 1.

This gives us the prime rule of doubling – if you can expect to win 25% of the time from any specific position then you can (and should) accept a double.

There is a second key point to be made here. Notice that with the introduction of doubling it is no longer necessary to get to the end of a game and bear off all your checkers first to win. Now all you need to do is get to a point where you have a greater than 75% chance to win the game, offer your opponent a double, and he will have to drop.

For those of you who have played or watched American Football the analogy is that you no longer actually have to score a touchdown to win the game; all you need to do is get to your opponent's 25-yd line.

(Note that the doubling cube can be used in any game. I have played chess and Scrabble with a doubling cube and I once watched a round of golf in which the doubling cube was in use - a five-figure sum changed hands at the eighteenth.)

Practical Examples

Let's look at a few simple examples. We start with endings because there are few checkers on the board and we can use our backgammon arithmetic to calculate some of the answers.

Example 1:

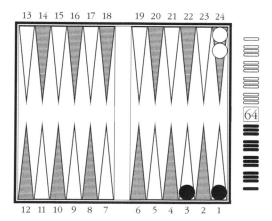

Here Black is on roll and he will win the game 34 times of 36. (Notice that when we analyse a position we often evaluate it in terms of 36 games as 36 is the number of possible rolls of the dice.)

Only when Black rolls 12 or 21 will he lose. Without the doubling cube, he will win 34 out of 36 games, or 94.4% of the time. With the doubling cube in play, however, Black will offer a double which White must decline - he is nowhere near the 25% he needs to take. Thus we see one of the key impacts of the cube – it reduces the element of luck.

Example 2:

Varying the position slightly:

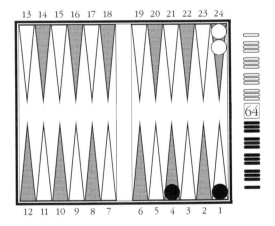

How often does Black win from here? He loses when he rolls 11, 12, 21, 13, 31, 23 or 32. This is 7 rolls and thus he wins 29 out of 36 times (80.6%). Again, Black will double and White must drop.

Example 3:

Another small change:

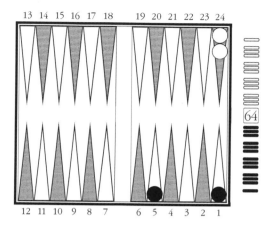

Black will win with 23 out of a possible 36 rolls – I will leave you to work out which rolls win and which lose. Now we have reached a point where Black will double but White will take. Doing the arithmetic:

In 36 games:

- If White drops he will lose 36 x (-1) = -36

- If White takes he will lose 23 x (-2) = -46

               but win 13 x (+2) = +26 for a net loss of -20

Thus White is better off taking than dropping.

These have all been what are called 'last roll' positions where Black's roll will decide the outcome of the game. On the last roll of the game it is correct to double with any advantage at all and if the opponent has 25% or better winning chances he will take. The standard reference position is shown below:

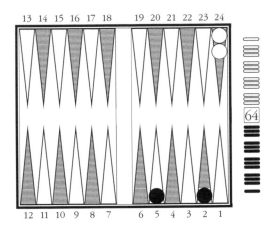

Here Black is only a 19/36 (52.8%) favourite yet it is still correct to double.

What if Black is not certain to win on his next roll – how does that change things?

Example 4:

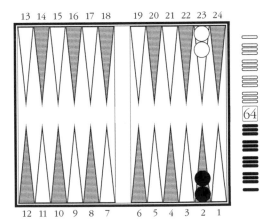

This is another well-known reference position. On Black's next roll he will win unless he rolls a 1, except double one. That means he will win 26/36 (72%) of the time on his roll so he should certainly double.

At first glance it looks as if White should drop the double because even when he does get to roll he only wins 26/36 of the time. His overall chances of winning are therefore 28% (Black misses) x 72% (White does not miss) which is only 20% - well below the 25% chance he needs.

However, we have overlooked a vital factor. Whenever Black fails to bear off his two checkers White will **redouble** to 4 before he rolls. Although he still wins only 20% of the time, he will have many more wins than losses for 4 points rather than 2 points. Without showing the maths here, that difference is enough to turn what would be a drop into a take.

This gives another of the fundamental lessons of doubling:

Owning the doubling cube is worth something and the longer there is to go in a game (and hence the more time you have to turn it round) the more valuable that ownership becomes.

This ownership is generally reckoned to be worth an additional 10% of a player's residual winning chances. 10% of 25%, the basic take point, is 2.5% so, rather than needing exactly 25% chances to take, the more general figure used by the majority of players is the range 22% to 23%.

If you are having trouble with all these percentages think of it this way:

In simple terms, ask yourself this: if I had this position repeatedly would I expect to win at least somewhere between 1 in 4 and 1 in 5 times? If yes, you have a take.

General Guidance

There are three fundamental questions with regard to doubling:

- When should I double?
- When should I redouble?
- When should I take and when should I drop?

In percentage terms these questions are relatively easy to answer. In very broad terms you need to be (at least) about a 66-67% favourite to double and close to 70% to redouble. The reason for the difference is that when you double both players have access to the cube. When you redouble you are giving away something you exclusively own and therefore you need to be slightly stronger to redouble than to give an initial double. As we have seen, 25% is the break-even point for taking/dropping and this should be adjusted downwards slightly for cube ownership.

The problem with backgammon is that except in endings these percentages are virtually impossible to calculate accurately. To get anywhere near the answer we have to combine two elements. Firstly we use the arithmetic which we have already discussed. Secondly, and much more importantly, we must remember that backgammon is a game of pattern recognition. In the same way that types of positions repeat themselves, then so also do doubling decisions.

If we had to treat each position as totally new we could be there for hours trying to work out the percentages listed above. Luckily, as you play the game you build a store of reference positions and you can call on these to help inform your doubling/taking decisions.

We will return to these topics in more depth in Chapter 10 but for now let me make some general points:

- **Taking/dropping is a reactive decision because it is your opponent who initiates the action.** The need to make a decision is forced upon you by your opponent.

- **Doubling/redoubling is a proactive decision because you initiate the action.** How to decide when to double/redouble is the most difficult thing in backgammon.

- **Most doubling/redoubling/taking decisions are based on a mixture of pattern recognition and calculation; the majority are made on pattern recognition.** This means that you have to build a good store of reference positions before you can become a really strong player.

- **You will make many checker plays during a single game of backgammon – you will only make one or two doubling decisions. Therefore – TAKE YOUR TIME.** Doubling is complex so make sure you spend enough time studying a position before you make your decision. As Paul Magriel said in his 1976 book 'Backgammon' - "Good checker play will never compensate for serious errors of judgement in doubling."

Summary

The basic mathematics of doubling is quite straightforward and must be understood by anyone aspiring to play the game well. As ever the devil is in the detail and even nearly ninety years after its introduction we still do not completely understand it.

To see how slowly we learn, look at this comment by Georges Mabardi, an eminent player of the day, writing in 1930, some four to five years after doubling was introduced: "If two absolutely perfect players engaged in a match, there would never be an accepted double." This is dramatically inaccurate but no doubt many of his readers in 1930 accepted it as gospel.

Doubling is very complex because pattern recognition, arithmetic, cube ownership, psychology, gammons and backgammons all play their part in the decision-making process.

This chapter has been a simple introduction. We will develop these basic themes in the next two chapters.

Chapter 9: Races and Endings

Races

Although backgammon is a complex game, ultimately it is a race. The two opposing armies eventually lose contact with each other – this happens when no further hitting is possible - and whichever player gets his checkers off first wins the game.

There is not a great deal of skill required to move the checkers in a pure race. Your job is to bring your checkers into your home board and then bear them off. Following these simple rules will assist you:

- Bring your checkers into your home board as quickly as possible (after all you can't bear them off until they are all home) but note that it is often better to fill a gap (especially on the 5- or 4-pt) than to bring a checker in.
- As you bear in to your home board put more checkers on the high points (6-pt, 5-pt, 4-pt) than the lower points. Avoid where possible having more than 2 checkers on your 1-pt or 2-pt.
- The 'ideal' structure for your checkers at the start of the bear-off is seven on your 6-pt, five on your 5-pt and three on your 3-pt.
- In the main take your checkers off according to the dice you roll. There is the odd exception but they are rare.

The key to races is understanding when to double/redouble and when to take/drop. It is therefore vital that we understand how to evaluate the race – how do we calculate who is winning? I apologise to those of you who do not like arithmetic but to understand races and make correct doubling decisions I am afraid that some further elementary maths will be required.

From a historical perspective none of the books from the popular 1930s era contained any useful information on this topic so I am not sure how our forebears coped with races other than by guesswork. Until the 1970s there were no decent racing formulae and the vast majority of backgammon players would not have known a pip count if they had met one. With the surge of interest that took place in the 1970s some order was finally imposed and the first rudimentary formula based on the pip count appeared.

What is a pip count? It is the number of pips you must roll with the dice to bear off all your remaining men. The pip count in the starting position is 167 for each side.

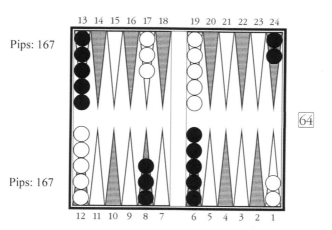

The pip count is calculated by multiplying the number of checkers on each point by the value of the point and summing the total.

In the diagram above Black's count is:

$(2 \times 24) + (5 \times 13) + (3 \times 8) + (5 \times 6) = 48 + 65 + 24 + 30 = 167$

Note: A checker on the bar is counted as 25 pips.

All diagrams from now on will show the pip count for both players as demonstrated in the diagram above.

We start by defining the two pip counts:

Leader's Pip Count (L): The number of pips required by the leader to bear off all his men.

Trailer's Pip Count (T): The number of pips required by the trailer to bear off all his men.

To help understand racing formulae a simple diagram is required. The line below shows the Trailer's pip count minus the Leader's pip count (T-L). Some of the key points on that line are highlighted:

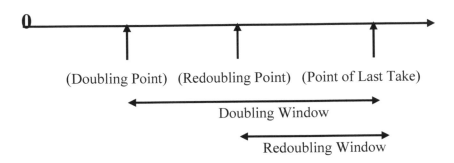

Some further definitions:

Doubling Point: The leader's lead in the pip count is just sufficient for him to offer an initial double.

Redoubling Point: The leader's lead in the pip count is just sufficient for him to offer a redouble.

Point of Last Take: The point at which the difference in the pip counts is such that the trailer still has a take but only just. Any increase in the difference would mean that the trailer must drop a double/redouble.

Doubling Window: The range of pip count difference within which double/take is the correct cube action.

Redoubling Window: The range of pip count difference within which redouble/take is the correct cube action.

The formula that we are going to use to assist us in our decision-making is simple but for all that it is reasonably effective and certainly a huge step forward from the visual inspection techniques that preceded it:

Let the leader's pip count be L.
Let the trailer's pip count be T.

If T is 8%   greater than L then the Leader should double.
If T is 9%   greater than L then the Leader should redouble.
If T is 12% greater than L then the Trailer should pass the double or redouble.

We will try this out on a simple position:

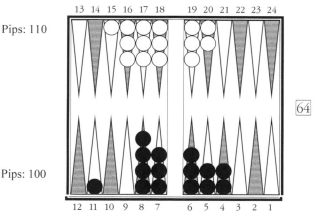

Pips: 110

Pips: 100

First, the pip counts:

Black's is $(1 \times 11) + (4 \times 8) + (3 \times 7) + (3 \times 6) + (2 \times 5) + (2 \times 4) = 11 + 32 + 21 + 18 + 10 + 8 = 100$

White's is $(1 \times 10) + (3 \times 9) + (3 \times 8) + (3 \times 7) + (3 \times 6) + (2 \times 5) = 10 + 27 + 24 + 21 + 18 + 10 = 110$

At first sight it might seem daunting to have to do this sort of arithmetic but, believe me, after a few months of play it becomes second nature. By dint of genetics and education some people will always be quicker than others at mental arithmetic but don't worry – just take your time and the more you play the quicker you will become.

Now apply our formula:

The Leader's pip count L is 100. The Trailer's pip count T is 110.

T is therefore 10% greater than L.

Applying the formula we notice that T is more than 8% or 9% greater than L so Black has a perfectly correct double and if he already owns the doubling cube he should also redouble. What about the take? White is less than 12% behind so he should take.

Changing the position slightly:

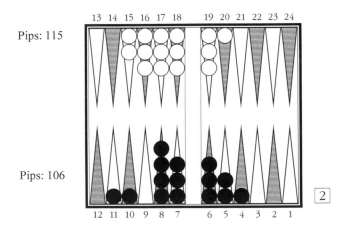

Pips: 115

Pips: 106

I'll leave you to check that my pip counts are correct. Now let's do the arithmetic.

We have L = 106 and T = 115

8% of 106 = 8.5 (approximately)
9% of 106 = 9.5 (approximately)
12% of 106 = 12.7 (approximately)

Black's actual lead in the race is 9 pips.

If we apply the formula we see that Black is strong enough to offer an initial double but is just shy of being able to redouble. As he owns the doubling cube he should not redouble. If Black were to double White has a very easy take (meaning that he is well inside the doubling window). As an exercise I would suggest setting up some positions like the ones above and practise doing the pip counts and then working out the correct doubling actions for both players.

This formula, while very basic, works well for long races and it is a good guide for all races where the pip counts are greater than 50 (below that the distribution of the checkers normally, but not always, begins to exert a greater influence).

If you have a lot of trouble with the arithmetic then you can be slightly more general in your approach. Notice the doubling window centres around a 10% lead and 10% is always easy to calculate.

Roughly two more pips than a 10% advantage for the leader means the trailer has a close take/drop decision. Two pips short of a 10% advantage for the leader and he has a borderline double; one pip short of a 10% advantage and he has a borderline redouble. This works well for most medium to long races, those within the 50 – 130 pips range (races greater than 130 pips are very unusual).

This is all I will say about racing formulae in this book. There are more sophisticated formulae which are more accurate because they take account of particular features of each player's checkers. These features are:

- Stacked points - points with many checkers on them
- Gaps - points with no checkers on them

- Extra checkers - in lots of races one player will already have borne off more checkers than his opponent
- Crossover – a crossover occurs when we move a checker from one quadrant of the board to another. If you have a high crossover count to get your checkers into your home board this can reduce your racing chances.

These other formulae are beyond the scope of this book but Walter Trice's "Backgammon Boot Camp" covers the topic in great detail.

Close races are the very life-blood of backgammon and I will illustrate that with a real example taken from the final of the 2003 World Championships.

That year's World Championship final was contested by Moshe Tissona of Israel and Jon Røyset of Norway.

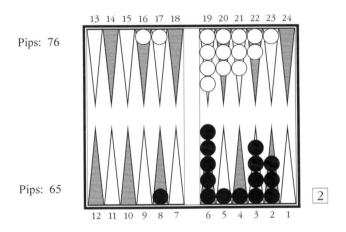

In a match to 25 points the two were tied at 17-17. The next game was pivotal. Early on Røyset (White) had the advantage and doubled his opponent but gradually Tissona turned the game round. When he threw three sets of double fives to take the lead in the race the position above was reached with Tissona (Black) on roll. He redoubled and Røyset pondered.

The bookmaker who had taken a 400 Euro bet on Tissona at 400-1 before the tournament started was looking pale. The crowd of some three hundred watching on closed circuit TV were calling on Røyset to pass. And still he pondered. After ten minutes he accepted the redouble.

The crowd couldn't believe it - the bookmaker's colour went off the scale. Credibility was stretched to breaking point when after double two from Black, bearing three checkers off, Røyset threw boxes (double sixes) - pandemonium!! Four rolls later he rolled double fives and claimed 4 points.

Tissona was broken and the rest of the match, though not without its moments, was something of an anti-climax, Røyset winning 25-20.

Now the key question – was it a take? Using the more sophisticated formulae available to experts it can be calculated that this position is a drop but only by the very tiniest of margins (computer analysis confirms this) and it is so close that nobody should be criticised for making the wrong decision. On the pip count alone it would be a clear drop but White's better checker distribution very nearly turns it into a take. Congratulations to Jon Røyset for having the courage to take the redouble under extreme pressure and reaping the reward when his opponent collapsed after losing this game.

Endings

When we get near to the end of the game we can no longer use racing formulae and have to resort to other methods including some of the simple arithmetic we used in the preceding chapter. How about this position?

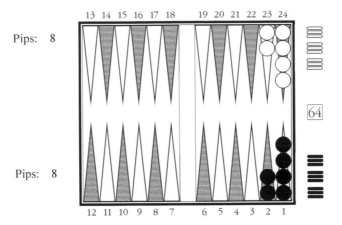

This is known as a 3-roll position, that is, if neither side rolls a double they will bear off their checkers in three rolls. Notice that if both players had five checkers instead of six it would make no difference. Unless White rolls a double in his next two rolls (assuming Black doesn't roll one) then Black will win the game. How often does that happen? Not quite often enough for White to take if Black doubles. White wins just over 21% of the time and, importantly, never gets the chance to redouble.

This is a basic reference position. You don't need to know the maths, just learn the correct cube action. Obviously the correct cube action for positions with fewer checkers for each side where neither player can miss is also double/drop. Adding two checkers to each side:

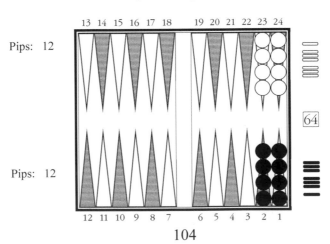

This is the standard 4-roll position (without rolling a double, each player requires four rolls to bear off). Now the game has longer to go, the correct cube action changes. Black should still double (or redouble) but now White can take. After the sequence non-double by Black, double by White and non-double by Black, White will be able to use the doubling cube to end the game as he will have a 2-roll position (4 checkers vs. 4 checkers) which is obviously a drop – thus he gets value from the doubling cube.

For positions of five or more rolls the correct cube action is double (but not redouble) and take. If Black already owns the cube he should wait until he reaches a 4-roll position and then redouble.

Unfortunately, backgammon is a game where you have to take account of small differences. Look at this position:

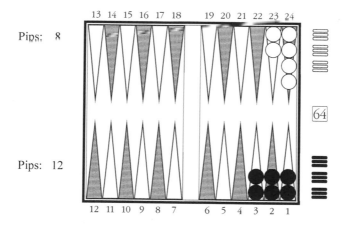

This looks like a 3-roll position so the correct cube action must be double/drop? Sadly not – the fact that Black might roll a 1 on each of his next three rolls is enough to turn what we thought was a drop into a very close take. There is no shortcut to learning this type of exception but once learnt the key is not to forget it and apply the same type of thinking to other positions.

Here is another example:

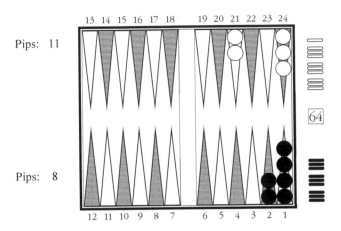

Pips: 11

Pips: 8

This time, for a change, White is on roll and doubles Black – should Black take? Again, it looks like a 3-roll position and in fact White has only 5 checkers so this must be a drop, mustn't it? The answer is no. Look what happens if White rolls 32 on his first roll – he won't bear off any checkers.

How often does that happen? 32 occurs twice in every thirty-six rolls (23 and 32) or approximately 5.5%. If we add that to the 21% chance of winning a 3-roll position then we get 26.5%, greater than the 25% we need to take.

Bill Robertie, twice world champion and prolific author, termed this the "Addition Method". Its principle is to calculate, as well as you can, the various ways of winning in a position and if that exceeds 25% you have a take. This takes practice and experience but I have used Robertie's method for years and it is an extremely useful tool.

This short section on endings has given you some basic reference positions and also introduced you to how to think about endings when there are only a few checkers left. You will learn a great deal more from actually playing and as you play you will increase your store of reference positions. Decision making will then become easier.

Bearing Off with Contact

So far we have only looked at positions where the two opposing armies have lost contact and are engaged in a pure race to the finishing line. What about the situation where your opponent still has checkers either in your home board or on the bar?

Dealing with the latter first:

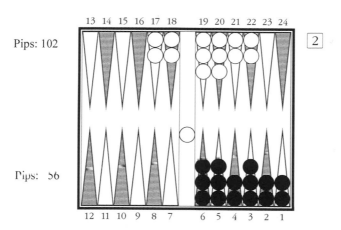

Here White has a checker trapped on the bar against Black's closed home board. He cannot play until Black opens one of his points, that is removes all, or all but one, of his checkers from that point. White can still win the game if Black is unlucky enough to leave a blot on a point and White subsequently hits that blot.

Black's strategy is to play safely and make sure he does not leave any blots unless the dice force him to do so. He should clear his points in order from the highest (his 6-pt). Additionally he should always try to keep an even number of checkers on his highest occupied point and ideally also on his two highest occupied points.

In the position above he is odd on his 6-pt (where he has three checkers) but even on the 5-pt and 6-pt (six checkers). However, notice that there is no roll of the dice that can force him to leave a blot next turn. One useful rule of thumb is that if you can play 66 safely then most or all rolls will play safely. Here 66 is played 6/off(3), 5/off which is fine.

If Black rolled 61 in this position he should play 6/off, 5/4 which leaves him even on the 6-pt and on the 5-pt and 6-pt combined (6/off, 3/2 would be an error). Once White has re-entered his checker, Black can start to bear off aggressively, that is as quickly as possible, but until then he must play with caution. After all he is winning the game comfortably and doesn't need to take risks.

How about when your opponent still owns a point in your home board such as in this position?

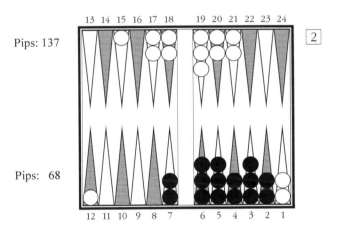

Here White owns Black's 1-point (often referred to as the ace point). Remember, when your opponent holds a point in your home board it is called an 'anchor'. This is much more dangerous for Black and despite his best efforts he is much more likely to leave an exposed blot. His plan is still to clear from the rear and then bear his checkers off. As with the previous position he should aim to stay even on his highest point and preferably on his two highest points together.

Unlike the previous position there is some immediate jeopardy. Look what happens if Black rolls 65. He cannot legally play the 6 and the only legal 5 is 7/2 which is the move he must make. Unfortunately for him this leaves a blot exposed on his bar-point and if White rolls a 6 next turn – remember he will do so 11 times out of 36 (31%) – then he will probably win the game.

Things could get even worse. Moving the game on a few rolls:

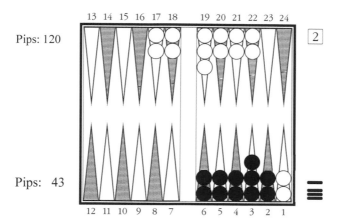

Pips: 120

Pips: 43

Now look at the impact of Black rolling 65. He has to play 6/off, 5/off leaving two blots! If White rolls a 5 or a 4 (56%) next turn he will have a winning position.

Despite the frustration that Black will feel when this happens, this type of sequence is exactly what makes backgammon so exciting. White, who was losing the game – and would probably lose a gammon from this position – suddenly turns the game round and finds himself in a winning position.

When bearing off against an anchor, the deeper in your home board the anchor is, the more likely you are to leave a shot. The case above, the ace-point anchor, generates the most shots for White whilst if he owns the 5-pt he will get very few shots.

One of the things you quickly learn in backgammon is that there are nearly always some winning chances in any position no matter how bad it is. If I had £1 for every person who has come up to me and started by saying, "you won't believe it but ....", I would be a very rich man indeed.

The ultimate 'last chance saloon' is known as the Coup Classique. Look at this position with White on roll:

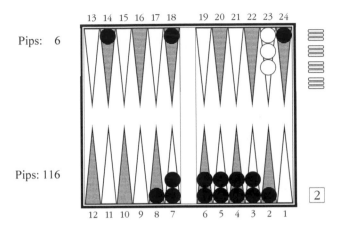

Believe it or not, there is still a lot of play in this position. Of course, if White rolls a double (other than 11) he will win a backgammon. If he rolls two numbers that do not contain a 1 then Black can hit the remaining checker with any 1 of his own. He should then be able to close out the single checker and save the gammon. In fact he will actually win the game 7% of the time.

The really interesting variation comes when White rolls a number containing a 1 (except 11), as he will have to leave blots on both his 1- and 2- points and Black will have a checker on the bar. Should Black then roll a 1 or a 2 then the game is far from over.

The correct technique here is not simple but if Black closes out both of White's blots then he becomes a 68% favourite to win. He should not redouble, however, until he has taken off three men. There is something innately satisfying in bringing off the "Coup". Being on the wrong side of it can be seriously damaging to your psychological health.

Finally in this section let us look at doubling when you have managed to hit a late shot and then close out the hit checker. You will reach a position something like this:

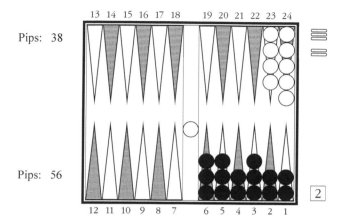

The question is when should Black redouble? The answer, which was first derived by Bill Robertie, is that you should redouble when you have taken off five fewer checkers than your opponent. Here Black has taken no checkers off and White has borne off five. This is Black's optimal redoubling point.

The 'five checkers off' idea should only be used as a guide and not as a fixed rule. If, for example, White had five checkers on his 3-pt instead of his 1-pt then the correct action here would be redouble/drop. The reason is that, once White enters his checker from the bar and then brings that checker home again, he will not bear off checkers when he rolls 1's. This is enough to turn a take into a drop.

Chapter 10: Advanced Doubling

In Chapter 8 we looked at the basics of doubling. Although the preceding chapter was on races and endings we somehow found ourselves discussing doubling decisions as well. That is because doubling is intrinsic to backgammon and in the majority of positions we need to take account of the doubling cube in making our decisions.

Firstly we look at the impact of gammons and backgammons in deciding whether or not take a double.

The Gammon Factor

An additional rule of backgammon that is played universally in money games but never in tournaments is the Jacoby Rule - named after the bridge and backgammon master, Oswald Jacoby. This states:

"You cannot win a gammon or a backgammon unless the doubling cube has been turned."

The reason for the rule is to speed up the game. Early in a game one player may get an overwhelming advantage where his opponent would have a very clear drop if doubled. To stop the winning player taking many more moves to try for the gammon win, the Jacoby Rule was introduced to force the player to take his one point win and move on to the next game.

The humour comes when the winning player offers the double and the losing player accepts it anyway – this happens more often than you would think.

Now what about the influence of gammons? (We will ignore backgammons as they occur about once in every 100 games and won't have any effect on our thinking.)

How often do gammons happen? Expert opinion is divided but the figure is somewhere between 20% and 26%. Of all games played to a conclusion, that is, not ended prematurely by a dropped double, between 1 in 4 and 1 in 5 end in a gammon for the winning side. That's quite a high percentage.

This means that if we are considering accepting a double in a typical middle game position such as this one we need to consider gammons.

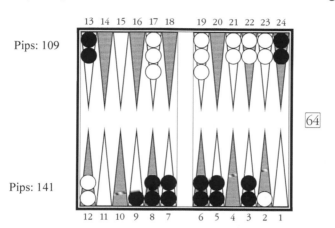

Let us look at the impact of gammons. We accept the double so the cube is on 2. Losing a single game costs us 2 points; losing a gammon costs us 4 points. But if we turn the game round and win then we win 2 points. So compared with losing a single game, we are 4 points better off if we win and only 2 points worse off if we lose a gammon.

This simple arithmetic shows that winning the game is twice as good as losing the gammon is bad. This gives us a simple guideline as to how we should alter our take percentage to allow for gammons.

You will remember from our earlier work that when we were not considering gammons we established our general take point as 22-23%.

For every gammon that we lose we must win an extra half-game (over and above the 'standard' 22-23%) to compensate. To look it

113

another way, if we believe that in a given position we are going to lose a gammon 20% of the time then we need 10% extra wins to compensate for the loss of those gammons.

If a position has its 'standard' gammon potential of 20% then that take point rises to 32-33%.

Looking at this in simple terms the question you now need to ask yourself is:

"Can I expect to win this game 1 time in 3? If so, I have a take, if not then I must drop the double."

Estimating the gammon potential of a position is difficult and only comes with practice. For those who have played very little, the 1 in 3 question is a good starting point.

On the other side of the coin a strong gammon threat can turn a marginal double into a very strong one. Psychologically the threat of winning a gammon is very powerful and should be used to good effect. I have seen many an opponent drop a perfectly acceptable double purely because he or she was frightened of losing a gammon.

Doubling Elements

Now we enter the most difficult area of doubling. How do we decide when to double/redouble? This discussion of percentages is all very well but the vast majority of positions cannot be analysed in this way. As I said earlier we have to rely to a large extent on pattern recognition and our store of reference positions. To these we add, when we can, specific tactical considerations such as whether we can attack a blot and if so how many numbers hit.

Can we break a backgammon position down into elements that we can understand on a regular basis? The answer is yes, although often we are left with subjective rather than objective analysis. There are three fundamental elements:

The Race

- Who leads in the race? After all, backgammon is fundamentally a race and most of the time the person who leads the race is winning the game.

Threat

- Are you threatening to improve your position by:

  ➤ Making new points?
  ➤ Hitting your opponent's blot(s)?
  ➤ Bringing your last checker home safely?

Position

- Who has the better static elements such as:

  ➤ Number of home board points?
  ➤ Prime or potential prime?
  ➤ Connectivity?
  ➤ Gammon potential?
  ➤ Anchor in the opponent's board?

Hopefully, having read this far, most of these points are self-explanatory. The one we have not discussed is connectivity. Briefly, backgammon checkers work better when they are close to each other. For example, at the start of the game the two checkers on our opponent's ace-point are 11 pips away from their nearest companions. That is why we make such an effort to get them moving as quickly as possible in the opening. Bill Robertie covers this topic in depth in his excellent book "Modern Backgammon".

These three elements, race, threat and position, are what you need to evaluate any problem. Sometimes it is easy and sometimes, by the very nature of the game, it is extremely difficult.

The broad rule of thumb is that you should at least be considering doubling/ redoubling if you have the advantage in two of the three elements. Like all rules of thumb you have to temper your analysis with experience and judgement.

When you first start to play, your pattern recognition ability will be limited and your store of reference positions will be small. You will make mistakes. Accept this as part of the learning process and you will soon improve. This need to build a store of knowledge is one of the reasons we do not get child prodigies in backgammon – it takes a while to build your knowledge base.

By the way the process never stops. You continue to refine your knowledge until the day you give up the game – for most players this coincides with a visit from the grim reaper.

Here are a couple of positions to reinforce this approach:

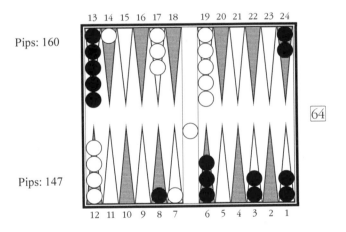

Pips: 160

Pips: 147

This is a very early game position but already Black has a huge advantage:

Race	- he leads by 13 pips
Threat	- two blots to aim at and one already on the bar
Position	- he has three home board points and a good chance to win a gammon

It should be clear that Black has a powerful double and I hope equally clear that White should drop.

At the other end of the spectrum:

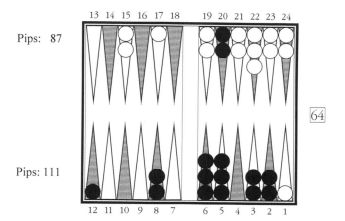

Pips: 87

Pips: 111

Black is on roll. Looking at the three elements:

Race	Black trails by 24 pips
Threat	Black has two blots to attack (on his 17-pt and his ace-point). He is also threatening to improve his blockade by making either his bar-pt or his 4-pt.
Position	White has a slightly stronger home board (five points made to Black's four) but he has a checker stranded on Black's ace-point (such a checker is known as a straggler).

Should Black be doubling? He is ahead in threat and behind in the race. The position element is in the balance. Some players would double and others would wait. Later in this chapter we will discuss an approach that we can use to decide on the correct cube action.

By applying a little rigour to analysing positions we have defined a method that will at least give us some idea of whether we should be doubling or not.

One very key consideration that is crucial to the whole doubling process is this:

EVERY ROLL IS A NEW DOUBLING DECISION

Even if your position was not strong enough to double last turn, do not assume it is not strong enough this turn. Before rolling the dice you should always ask yourself the question – should I be doubling?

This brings us nicely to the topic of volatility.

Volatility

In some backgammon games the advantage to one player or the other develops very slowly. In others the change can come very quickly, for example, the hit of a blot followed by the opponent fanning (fanning is a term used for failing to enter from the bar).

This measure of the speed of change is called volatility. Again we will consider the two ends of the spectrum.

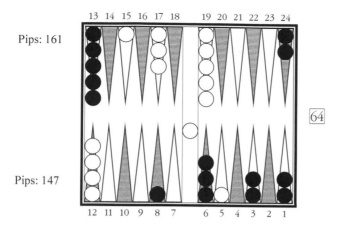

Pips: 161

Pips: 147

64

This is another early game where White opened with 43, played 24/20, 13/10. Black responded with 55 played 8/3(2), 6/1(2)*. White then fanned with 66.

The position is extremely volatile and Black's next roll will have a huge impact on the outcome. For example, if Black rolls 63 he will play 24/15*. If White then fans again he must drop Black's double. For this reason Black must double before he rolls – by next turn White may no longer be able to take a double.

If Black does not double he is likely to experience what is called a 'Market Losing Sequence'. Two rolls, one by him and one by his opponent, have caused such a change in the position that the doubling action has changed.

In backgammon, you want to avoid 'Market Losing Sequences'. The higher the volatility of a position, the more market losing sequences there are likely to be. Losing your market by a small margin is not a problem but if you significantly overshoot the target you will have cost yourself money or points.

In Chapter 8 I used the analogy of American Football and explained that the target was your opponent's 25-yard line. Continuing the analogy, reaching the 21-yard line before you double is no great sin but if you find yourself on the 5-yard line and you have not doubled then that is definitely a mistake.

119

Now we will look at a non-volatile position:

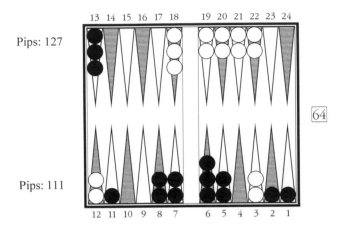

Pips: 127

Pips: 111

64

Here White owns an anchor in Black's board and Black is trying to bring all his checkers safely into his home board. Black leads in the race but has few if any threats and the positions are nearly equal. There are virtually no market losing sequences and Black should not double.

This gives us another good guideline. **If there are no market losing sequences in a position, it is never correct to double.**

If, after your roll and your opponent's, your position has got worse, you will be glad you did not double. If it has got better you can consider offering a double on your next turn. Remember – every roll is a new doubling decision.

Woolsey's Law

In our discussion of doubling elements the following position left us in a quandary as to whether or not to double:

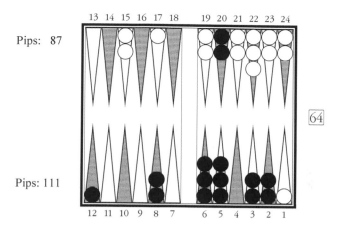

Pips: 87

Pips: 111

64

How can we solve this problem?

Many years ago Kit Woolsey, who had come to backgammon via chess and bridge, asked himself the same question. He found that quite often in his games he was losing his market and instead of winning two or four points he was winning a paltry single point when his opponents kept dropping his doubles.

To solve this problem he developed Woolsey's Law which goes as follows:

Ask yourself the following question:

     If I were doubled in my opponent's position, is it a take?

There are three possible answers:

       a. Yes, I'm absolutely sure it is a take
       b. No, I'm absolutely sure it is a pass
       c. I'm not 100% sure

Woolsey's Law then states:

If the answer is (c) then it is ALWAYS correct to double.

Let's see how this works:

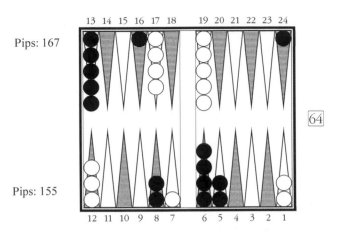

Pips: 167

Pips: 155

64

Here the game is only a few moves old but already Black has some advantages: he has a better home board, he has a White blot on his bar-point to attack, he has partially escaped one of his back checkers and he leads in the race.

By our criteria he is ahead in our three elements and should be considering doubling. The position is quite volatile with several market losing sequences available. It looks like a double. Now apply Woolsey's Law – should White take? If there is any doubt in your mind at all then you, as Black, must double and, crucially, give the problem to your opponent.

When Woolsey first started using his law he suddenly found he was winning a lot more money because he was winning gammons instead of single games. It also baffled his opponents that in quite complex positions he would only take 10-15 seconds to decide to double. This was because he had evaluated the position and decided he didn't know 100% whether it was a take. That was enough for him – across came the cube!

Why does Woolsey's Law work? Let Kit explain in his own words:

"If there is some doubt in your mind as to whether it is a take or not, there are several possibilities:

a) Maybe it actually is a pass. I hope most people are sophisticated enough to realize that if you fail to turn the cube when your opponent's correct action is to pass you are potentially costing yourself a lot of money, regardless of what your opponent will actually do.

b) Maybe your opponent will think it is a pass. If there is ANY doubt in your mind, then there is always a possibility that your opponent may view his position more pessimistically than you and choose to pass the double. If you fail to double in such a position you have given your opponent a free roll to get back in the game when you could have collected a sure point, which is extremely expensive.

c) Maybe it is a correct double, even if it is a take and your opponent correctly takes. This is not an unlikely scenario. The fact that you thought there was some possibility that it might be a pass indicates that your position is strong and there are undoubtedly a few market losing sequences. If this is the case, it could easily be correct to double even if your opponent is correctly taking.

d) Worst case – It is not theoretically correct to double, and your opponent correctly takes. How bad is this? Not very bad. Unless your assessment of the position is completely off base you still have a clear advantage – how bad can that be? You will only regret your decision to double if he turns the game around – then you will lose twice as much as if you hadn't doubled. Since you are the favourite in the game, things are not all that bad.

Does this law apply only to initial doubles, or does it apply to redoubles as well? Surprisingly enough, it applies just as strongly to redoubles, for all the same reasons. It is true that it is more costly to sacrifice a cube that you own than to sacrifice a centre cube when you err and make a theoretically incorrect redouble (and your opponent correctly takes, which he might not), but in the long run you will still gain by using the law for redoubles as well as initial doubles."

I have used Woolsey's Law ever since I first read about it and believe me it is the most useful doubling aid there is. It never ceases to amaze me how often people drop when I was not even sure I should be doubling so a big thank you to Kit for all the extra points he has won for me over the years.

The Psychology of Doubling

The psychology of doubling is a topic on which it would be easy to write a book. For now a few key points will suffice.

Never forget you are playing a human being (at least most of the time). What is a clear take to you might be a clear pass to him. In any session against an unknown opponent you should test him early with some aggressive cubes – you will be surprised how often you get a drop you were not expecting. As the session develops you will get a feel for your opponent's cube handling skills and you should tune your own doubling habits based upon what you learn.

Many beginners wait far too long to double. Hopefully the application of Woolsey's Law will help you to overcome that particular problem.

Many years ago the American expert Kent Goulding would give his students a position and ask them if they would double. Often they would say no. Three or four weeks later he would give them the same position but playing the other side and ask them if they would accept a double. Again the answer was no! Something is wrong somewhere. The implication is that many players underestimate their winning chances both when doubling and taking.

"I didn't double because I thought he might take" is a phrase I have heard rather more often than I would like. The vast majority of correct early and middle game doubles are also perfectly correct takes so do not be afraid to double.

Too Good to Double

In our discussions so far we have covered these four scenarios:

Player 1 Cube Decision	Player 2 Cube Decision
1. Not good enough to double	Take
2. Double	Take
3. Redouble	Take
4. Double/redouble	Drop

There is one more situation that we need to cover and that is when a player becomes too good to double. Here is a simple example:

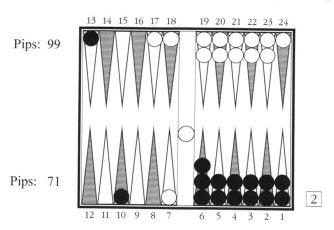

Black has one of White's checkers closed out and has many shots at the other White blot on his bar-point. Note that he also owns the cube on 2. Obviously if he redoubles White will drop like a shot and be grateful to lose only two points.

Black's correct strategy should be to try to hit the second blot and then to play on for the gammon and win four points. Of course he may never hit the second blot, e.g. if his first roll is 55, but even with one checker closed out the correct strategy is to play on for the gammon until there is some significant risk of losing the game.

Where is the break point? Again, the arithmetic is simple. If we turn a single win (with the cube on 2) into a gammon we gain two extra points. If we turn a win into a loss we lose four points (losing two instead of wining two points). Therefore to play on for the gammon we need to be twice as likely to win a gammon as we are to lose the game.

In the above position Black will win a gammon 50% of the time and lose 5% of the time so he is ten times more likely to win a gammon than to lose the game. Therefore he should play on. But note that, as with all doubling decisions, each roll is a new decision and a position may change from being one that is too good to double to one where the player should cash (because the 2-1 odds for playing on no longer exist) – in backgammon 'cashing' means doubling in the sure knowledge that the opponent will drop.

Thus we complete our table above as follows:

Player 1 Cube Decision	Player 2 Cube Decision
1. Not good enough to double	Take
2. Double	Take
3. Redouble	Take
4. Double/redouble	Drop
5. Too good to double/redouble	Drop

This completes the full spectrum of basic doubling decisions but before we leave the topic we need to discuss three more things.

Beaver

What happens if your opponent doubles you when you are the favourite in the position? The rules of backgammon allow you to beaver the double. You do this by turning the cube to 4 **but you keep the cube on your side of the board.** The player being beavered has the option of dropping the beaver, that is, he pays two points and starts a new game.

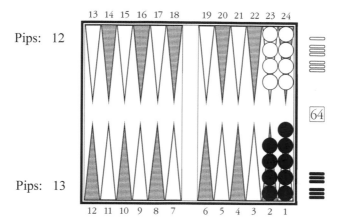

Pips: 12

Pips: 13

Here, Black miscounts his checkers and, thinking that both sides have eight checkers left, offers a double to White. White, realising Black's error, beavers the double (which Black should accept) and now the cube is on 4 on White's side of the board. If Black does not roll a double White will redouble to 8 on his next turn and Black will have a perfectly correct take. Beware - beavers can be expensive.

Beavers are only used in money games, never in tournaments.

Raccoon

What happens if the original doubler believes his double to be correct and it is the person who beavers that has made the mistake? The original doubler may then raccoon the beaver by turning the cube to 8. (The cube remains with the opponent.) Whilst beavers are nearly always allowed, raccoons are rarely played but they can add an additional level of excitement to the game.

Settlements

The cube can get to very high levels and in simple positions it is sometimes possible to work out a settlement.

127

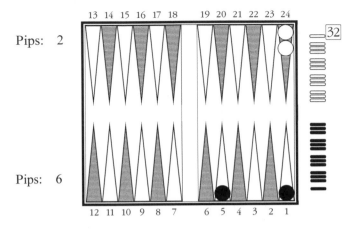

Pips: 2

Pips: 6

The cube is on 32 and the next roll will decide the game. Using our basic backgammon arithmetic we can calculate that Black will win 23 games and lose 13 (when he rolls 11, 12, 21, 13, 31, 14, 41, 24, 42, 23, 32, 34, 43).

Over 36 games he will win 23 x 32 points and lose 13 x 32 points. His net winnings will be 10 x 32 points. Dividing by 36 to get his average winnings per game we get a fraction under 9. If the players wish to settle the position rather than have Black roll then the 'fair settlement' would be for White to pay Black 9 points.

Of course, the players can haggle. White may offer to pay 8 and Black will counter demanding 10. After a little discussion they will probably – but not necessarily – agree on 9 points.

Summary

The doubling cube is complex but we have covered all the fundamentals. Although we have completed the chapters that are specifically about doubling, from now on we will encounter the doubling cube in most of our discussions as it is so intrinsic to the game.

Chapter 11: The Middle Game

Our next step is to look at the middle game. We have looked at the openings in some depth but each game develops from the opening into a middle game that might be very straightforward or might be highly complex. It is in the middle game that the majority of games are won or lost and where the most difficult doubling decisions are to be found. It would be possible to devote a chapter to each type of middle game but because of space limitations we will just look at the basics of each type and provide some straightforward guidelines.

Luckily for us, over the years players have come to understand that most middle games fall into one of a number of recognisable types. These types have names as follows:

- Running Game (Race)
- Mutual Holding
- High Anchor
- Low Anchor
- Blitz
- Prime versus Prime
- Back Game
- Scrambles
- Saving the Gammon

In this section we are going to define each type of game and then look at the playing and cube strategies it requires. To be successful at backgammon it is vital to get an understanding of these various game types

We have already covered races in Chapter 9 so we will start with Mutual Holding games.

Mutual Holding Game

A mutual holding game is one where each side has a high anchor (a high anchor is one of three points - your opponent's 4-pt, 5-pt or bar-point) such as the position below:

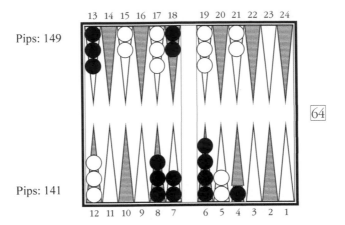

Pips: 149

Pips: 141

Other than races, this type of game is the easiest to play and the strategy for both sides is relatively simple. The game is often won by the player who is first to throw a useful set of doubles. The strategy for both sides has three elements that should be prioritised in the following order.

Firstly, safely disengage the back checkers - this can normally only be done when you throw doubles. Secondly, build blocking points in front of your opponent. For example, in the position above Black would like to build his 9, 10 or 11 points. Thirdly, build points in your home board. This last tactic becomes increasingly important as the two armies fail to disengage. A strong home board is a good deterrent to your opponent leaving with one checker from his anchor as, when the remaining checker is hit, the stronger your home board the more likely it is that the hit will prove fatal to your opponent.

Doubling strategy is also relatively straightforward and many games end with a double that is passed. Either one player throws a set of doubles which puts him way ahead in the race or else he leaves a shot which is fatal if hit, but probably wins the game if missed. In each of these cases the double is normally obvious and the decision to take or pass relatively clear-cut. As doubling decisions go, these are amongst the easiest and it is unusual to see bad cube errors in a mutual holding game.

High Anchor Game

A high anchor game is one where you have moved your back checkers at least as far as your mid-point whilst your opponent still holds either your 4-pt, 5-pt or bar-point. An example is shown in the position below:

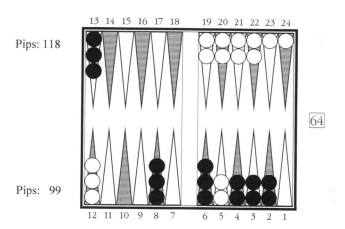

The game plans for the two sides in this position are quite clear. Black tries to bring all his checkers into his home board without leaving a shot. If he does have to leave a shot it will normally be on his mid-point after White has vacated his own mid-point, and White will therefore only have an indirect shot (a shot which requires a combination of the two dice) to hit and win the game.

Ideally, Black would like to throw a set of doubles and clear his mid-point without ever leaving a shot. White's strategy is slightly more complex as he has three objectives: keep the high anchor, keep the mid-point as long as possible and build a strong home board to ensure that if he does hit a loose Black checker he will win immediately. Of course a set of big doubles by White can put him right back in the race.

It is important that White builds his home board points in order (beginning with the 6-pt and then 5-pt, 4-pt, 3-pt and so on) as far as he can. He should slot points aggressively with the idea of building a strong home board as quickly as possible. He should hardly ever compromise his home board in order to keep his mid-point – he should prefer instead to let the mid-point go in order to keep a winning home board.

Doubling strategy is relatively straightforward. Black can double when he has slightly better than the equivalent of a racing double (i.e. a double based on the pip count alone). In a pure race Black can double with an 8% lead and White can take with up to a 12% deficit. In a typical high anchor position Black needs to have a racing lead of about 15% in order to double. High anchor positions are not very volatile as there are very few market losing sequences. Therefore Black should try to get to a point where he is very close to White's take/pass borderline before he doubles.

What is slightly surprising is that White can take with quite a large deficit in the pip count (up to 50 pips) because, as his chances of winning the race decrease, so his chances from winning by hitting increase. He will not be forced off his anchor prematurely so he can wait a long time for a shot. In the variations where his hitting chances are high it is imperative that he has a good home board; if he hasn't then what would be a take becomes a drop.

In the position above, the pip count is Black: 99 White: 118 so the correct cube action is for Black to double and White to take. As noted above White can be far worse off in the pip count and still have a take, as in this position:

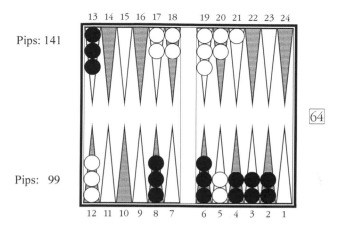

Pips: 141

Pips: 99

64

Now Black leads in the race by 42 pips but White still has a take. Note that White is correctly building a prime on his own side of the board. If he had a weaker home board structure, for example if he had already made his ace-point, then the position might be a pass.

As with many backgammon positions, small changes can lead to differences in doubling decisions. In the next diagram we have strengthened White's board by giving him his 4-pt but we have given Black his bar-point:

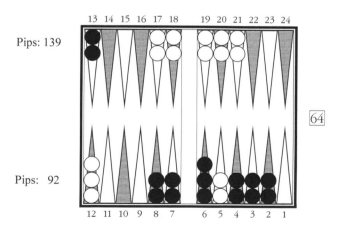

Pips: 139

Pips: 92

64

133

The change for Black has more influence than that for White. Now he has two landing points for his checkers on the mid-point so that a roll of 65 becomes a very good roll for him. This small change turns a clear take for White in the previous diagram to one that is now right on the take/drop borderline.

One of the most common decisions that confronts the player who is trying to bring his checkers home is how much risk should he take to clear his mid-point. Here is a classic example:

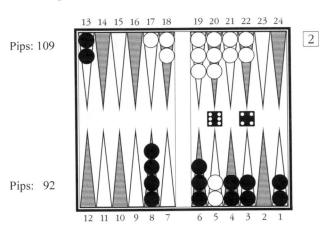

Black can play one checker from his mid-point with 13/3 and then hopefully bring the remaining blot to safety next turn. After that he should have an easy time bearing in the rest of his checkers from his 8-pt. However, White can immediately hit the blot that Black leaves with any 8 (6 numbers). Is the risk worth it?

This is known as a "Pay me now or pay me later problem". This theme recurs constantly in backgammon. In this position Black should play safely with 8/2, 8/4 and hope for a clearing double in the next couple of turns. As is often the case a small difference in the position can change the answer.

If Black had only two checkers on his 8-pt then 13/3 would be the right move as his position is deteriorating (he is running out of time to clear those outer points) and taking some risk is justified.

What about if White has a 4-pt anchor such as this?

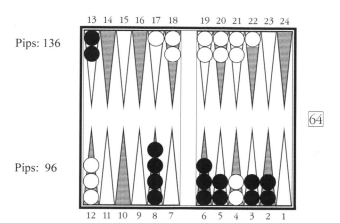

Pips: 136

Pips: 96

64

With a lower anchor White's racing chances diminish but his hitting chances increase. What we said about the 5-pt anchor holds true for the 4-pt anchor as well. Notice that clearing the mid-point becomes a little easier for Black. With a roll of 52 he brings two checkers down from the mid-point and leaves White only six hitting numbers (all the 7's).

In this position Black should double and White has a comfortable take.

Low Anchor Game

A low anchor game is one where one player holds his opponent's 1-, 2- or 3-pt. Each of them has slightly different characteristics and we will start with the 3-pt game. The 3-pt is a sort of half-way house between the high anchor game and what I call the true low anchor games – the 1-pt and 2-pt games.

As you would expect, the 3-pt game generates more hitting chances but fewer racing chances than a high anchor game. We have already seen a typical 3-pt game in Chapter 10. Here it is again:

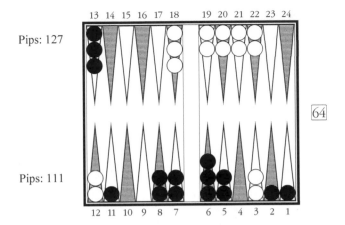

Pips: 127

Pips: 111

64

A 3-pt holding game is normally non-volatile and the advantage changes slowly from roll to roll. Black's only really good rolls in this position are 44, 55 and 66. With any other roll he will slowly bring his checkers home and will try to make his 4-pt if he possibly can.

White nearly has a take based on the race alone so it should be obvious that Black doesn't have a double here. Once Black makes his 4-pt he will have a double but even then White will have a take. There is an old adage in backgammon that any 3-pt game is a take. This is not quite true but it is very close. Note, however, that to be able to take a double White must preserve a strong home board – if he cannot contain a hit checker his winning chances drop dramatically.

The 2-pt and 1-pt games are subtly different. Now White will most often win by hitting a shot – he will be too far behind in the race to catch up. A second factor that must be considered is that if White cannot escape his back checkers at the appropriate moment he may well lose a gammon – this is especially true when White has more than two checkers on the anchor.

Here is a typical 2-pt game:

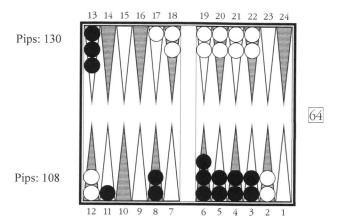

Pips: 130

Pips: 108

The vast majority of 2-pt and 1-pt games are doubles and passes, as is this one. White hits quite a few shots but often by the time he hits he has destroyed his home board, i.e. he has 12 or 13 checkers piled up on his 1-, 2- and 3-pts. Also, as noted he loses some gammons, more when he owns the 1-pt anchor than the 2-pt anchor.

What sort of change do we need to make to give White a take? Normally a take is based on a tactical opportunity.

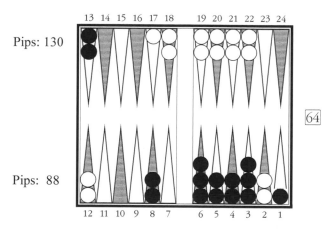

Pips: 130

Pips: 88

In the position above, Black has gained 20 pips in the race from our previous position but stands much worse. Why? The answer is that any roll containing a 6 other than 66 will leave an immediate shot.

137

These immediate hitting chances give White a take. This shows how important attention to detail can be in evaluating doubling decisions.

The 1-pt game generates far more shots than any other anchor – it is reckoned that if White stays to the bitter end he will get a shot 90% of the time. However, he has to hit that shot and contain the hit checker and, by the time he hits, Black may have already borne off ten or more checkers. Note also that White may elect to run for home in an effort to save the gammon rather than waiting for a last ditch shot. The 1-pt game generates fewer tactical chances than the 2-pt game and so in general terms is much worse than its bedfellow.

White may own the cube in a position like this:

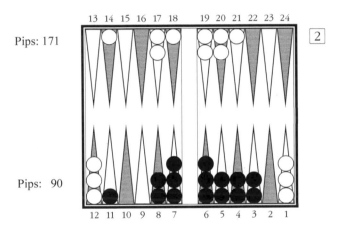

Pips: 171

Pips: 90

Now he has to follow the basic strategy for holding games – build his home points in order, try not to put any checkers out of play, that is more than two checkers on a lower home board point, and wait patiently for a shot.

Blitz

The blitz is the most volatile of all the game types. A blitz is characterised by one player desperately trying to get an anchor in his opponent's home board whilst his opponent does everything he can to prevent it. The position below is typical of the early stages of a blitz where White has split his checkers with a 52 played 13/8, 24/22 and Black has replied with 55, played 8/3(2)*, 6/1(2)* putting two White checkers on the bar.

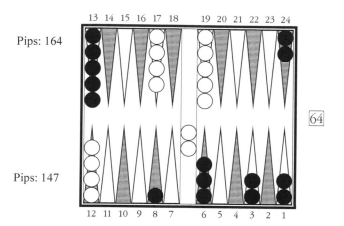

Pips: 164

Pips: 147

Should White fan then the game will be over. Black will double and White will drop. Quite often White will enter one checker whilst the other stays on the roof (a backgammon colloquialism for staying on the bar).

The strategies for the two players are clear. Black should keep hitting White whenever he can. Often he will have to leave a blot in his home board to do so. For example let us assume White brings one checker in by rolling 64, played bar/21.

If Black now rolls 32 he should play 13/10, 6/4* (6/4*/1 is not the right idea as Black should be trying to make new home board points). If he can't hit, Black should bring more checkers closer to the action, ready to hit next time. He should not worry about his back checkers, as there will be plenty of time to escape those later. Meanwhile White just has to hope that he can make an anchor. Having made it he should not give it up prematurely, but must patiently build up a strong home board, ready to contain a Black checker which White hopes to hit later.

Doubling strategy can be quite complex and must be learnt through experience. As soon as Black sees a good chance of a gammon he should be thinking of doubling – remember Woolsey's Law.

These early double 5 blitzes are well documented and understood. In particular you should read Kit Woolsey's (that man again) Backgammon Encyclopedia Volume 1. Middle game blitzes are much more difficult and less well understood.

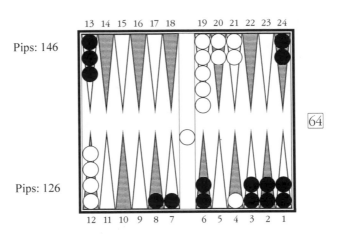

The position above is typical. Black has four home board points, two checkers ready to attack the White blot on his 4-pt and White has a checker on the bar – this adds up to a powerful combination.

It should be clear this is a highly volatile position and that Black should double now – by his next turn he could well have lost his market. Can White take? On the downside it is clear that when things go badly for him he will probably lose a gammon – is there an upside?

Yes there is and that is his home board. He has the three best points made and, crucially, has two Black checkers trapped behind them. If White can make an anchor in Black's board and/or hit a Black blot then that home board will come into its own. So much so that in fact this position is a very trivial take for White. The volatility does make it a double for Black but it is close. In the game from which this position was taken White dropped the double which was a massive blunder.

One final piece of advice: the defending side tends to be over-optimistic about its chances of making an anchor. If in doubt, drop a double - gammons are expensive.

Prime versus Prime

Prime versus prime is probably the most difficult of all game types to play although back games can also become very complex. Firstly what do we mean by prime versus prime? It is a position where each player has a prime (remember a prime is a set of contiguous points) of at least four points but normally five or six points (a six point prime is a full prime) and at least one enemy checker trapped behind the prime.

This position is a classic prime versus prime where each player has a five-prime with two of his opponent's checkers trapped.

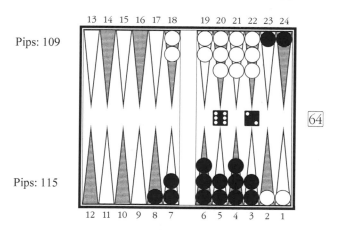

Pips: 109

Pips: 115

Prime versus prime games require finely honed judgement and a fair amount of experience to play well. In a race or a blitz, once you have embarked upon them, most of the moves are relatively straightforward. In a prime versus prime game each move will require much more thought.

The understanding and use of the doubling cube are critical to successful prime versus prime play. One of the reasons for this is that these games quite often end in a gammon for one side or the other. This is because one player's position suddenly collapses and he finds himself with two or more checkers closed out on the bar.

In terms of strategy there are three basic elements: if not already at the edge of your opponent's prime move up to the edge whenever you can; escape from behind your opponent's prime (known as leaping the prime) and finally hit your opponent away from the edge of your prime.

The position above is taken from my first book "Backgammon – An Independent View" and I mis-analysed it originally. Black has a 62 to play and I am pleased to be able to set the record straight here.

My original analysis made the classic error of studying two moves (a) 23/17, 8/6 and (b) 8/2*, 4/2 and choosing between them whilst simply overlooking that play (c) 23/17, 4/2* was an option.

Play (c) implements two of our three elements of strategy. It escapes a checker (23/17) and it knocks White away from the edge of Black's prime (4/2*). It is far stronger than either (a) or (b).

Interestingly my error highlights one of the most common errors in backgammon: trying to choose between Play A and Play B whilst not even noticing that Play C is an option. Sadly, it is a fact of life that we all miss moves from time to time. Not surprisingly the best players very seldom fail to see a move. They may reject a move through erroneous analysis but they will at least have considered it.

One of the key things to consider in prime versus prime games is the number of checkers that each side has trapped behind his opponent's prime. The more checkers trapped the worse the situation becomes.

Here is a potential prime versus prime game that is in the early stages of development:

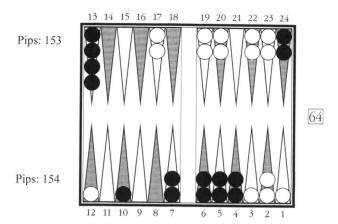

Black has 'only' a four-prime whilst White has a broken prime (a prime with gaps in it). However, White already has four checkers trapped behind Black's prime and if Black rolls a 1, 33 or 66 a fifth one will join the party. Although White does have a four-point home board, his position is already so weak that he must drop a double from Black.

This position reinforces a point that I made earlier and that is the connectivity of the checkers. They work better when they are relatively close together. In the position above, White's army is split into two and we know from history that armies that suffer this fate rarely win battles.

The problem with having several checkers trapped behind a prime is that they cannot move. Therefore rolls must be played by moving checkers elsewhere on the board and quite often you don't want to move those checkers. There is a word in chess, 'Zugzwang', which is used to describe a position where the player to move is at a disadvantage precisely because he has to move. Prime versus prime positions are often the backgammon equivalent of Zugzwang.

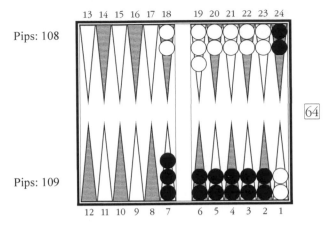

In this position whoever is to move is the underdog. Each side would like to keep its perfect full prime but if Black is on roll then only twenty rolls enable him to maintain that prime. Note that of those twenty rolls the best of all is 66 because he has no legal moves.

If you take the third checker from Black's bar-point and put it on his 17-pt he would be much better off as he could move that checker safely next turn and maintain his prime unless he were to roll 44 or 55. This gives Black what we call 'timing'. In backgammon, timing is defined as the number of pips a player can move without weakening his position.

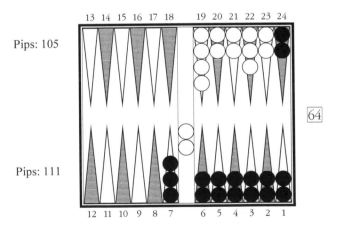

144

Prime versus prime games can also occur when one side has a checker (or checkers) closed out on the bar as in the example above.

If Black rolls a 6 next turn he will have a strong position and White will have to drop a double. However, give Black 54 followed by 44 and his home board will self-destruct. These positions can be balanced on a knife edge and you can go from overwhelming favourite to underdog in a very short space of time.

In this position Black should not double until he has escaped one back checker by rolling a 6 (while he still has a closed home board). White should then drop the double.

Learning how to handle the doubling cube well in such positions requires many hours of study and experience. Prime versus prime games often turn into back games so we shall study these next.

Back Game

In a back game one player holds two or more points in his opponent's home board, usually as a result of lots of blots being hit. Firstly, a really excellent piece of advice: AVOID back games at all costs. When they go well they are wonderful but, if you lose, then you are likely to lose either a gammon or a backgammon.

In the 1970s playing back games was all the rage but modern players actually like to come out ahead, so back games are now much rarer. Having said that, it is important to understand them and learn the correct strategies for playing them.

Here is a typical back game:

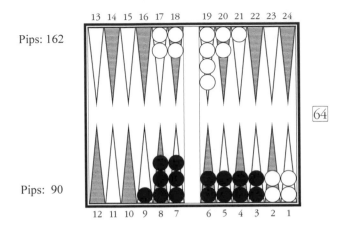

Pips: 162

Pips: 90

64

White holds Black's 1-pt and 2-pt. What are the strategies of the two players?

Black attempts to bear in and then bear off his checkers without leaving any shots. White meanwhile tries to build a strong home board, ready to contain any Black checker that he hits. The problem with White's strategy is that, like a prime versus prime game, a couple of bad rolls can destroy his position. Look at the impact of 55 followed by 44 in the position above – his home board will be destroyed as all his checkers pile up on his lower points.

This position also demonstrates the peculiarity of the 1-2 back game (back games are designated by the points held in the opponent's board). Once Black has borne in the checker from the 9-pt he will not have a legal six to play and so this will slow down his bear in. This is exactly the opposite of what White wants as he needs to get a shot and hit it whilst he still has a strong home board.

What about doubling strategy? For many years this was misunderstood and much erroneous advice was given. It wasn't until the advent of computers that we could get enough data to provide reasonably reliable advice. Analysis has recently shown that you should normally wait to double a back game until you have three points to clear in front of your opponent's highest anchor.

In the case of playing against a 1-2 back game that would imply you should clear the 6-pt before doubling. Whether your opponent has a take then depends on such factors as how your checkers are structured on the remaining three points (the 5-, 4- and 3-) and the state of his home board. As with prime versus prime games the back game player needs to keep his timing - he must be able to maintain his home board until he hits a shot.

What White wants is to end up with something like the next position and then have Black roll 64 exposing a blot on his 6-pt to a double shot – a double shot is a blot that can be hit by two direct numbers, in this case a 4 or a 5.

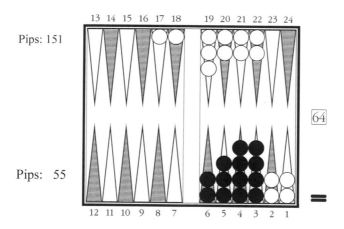

This position between Walter Cooke (Black) and Jesse Sammis (White) is one of the most famous in backgammon history. The score was 0-0 in a match to 17 points.

Cooke doubled this position (Black has already borne off two checkers), Sammis took, Cooke rolled 65 and Sammis promptly redoubled (incorrectly) to 4. When he missed the double shot Cooke put the pressure on by redoubling to 8, which Sammis took. When Sammis got a later double shot he redoubled to 16!

This time he hit, and the game was in the balance for a while, but Cooke looked to be home and dry when only a non-double by him followed by double sixes by Sammis could lose the game for him.

Cooke redoubled to 32. Recognising that being 16-0 down in a match to 17 was hopeless Sammis took the redouble. Cooke rolled an innocuous 42 and Sammis promptly rolled boxes (double sixes)!! An incredible game; but what about Cooke's initial double?

For many years most observers believed that Sammis had made an error by taking but modern analysis shows the take was correct. Note that, although he had four points to clear, Cooke's double was also correct because Sammis's timing was precarious – one bad roll could have destroyed his home board.

Which are the best points to hold for a back game? By far the best back games are the 2-3 and 1-3. After that come the 2-4, 3-4 and 1-4. The 1-2 game featured above actually generates the most shots but it is very difficult to time correctly – more often than not a rogue roll destroys White's plans.

The 3-5 and 4-5 back games are quite effective if the opponent has an 'outside' prime - one that extends from his 6-pt to his 11-pt. The 2-5 is a weak back game and the 1-5 is hardly a back game at all – it is usually viewed as a 5-pt holding game with extra chances.

Once the player who is conducting the back game gets his shot and hits it, his job is at best half done. He has to contain the hit checker, hit another one if he can, close out those checkers and then win the race. Quite often positions like this arise:

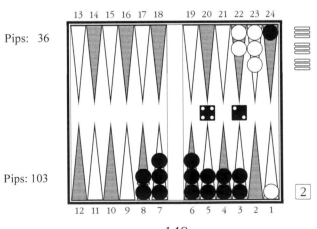

Pips: 36

Pips: 103

148

Black has played a back game, hit his shot and trapped a White checker behind his full prime. He now wants to close out the hit checker and ideally he would like to pick up another White blot which would virtually guarantee him the win. To that end he has left a checker for as long as he can in White's home board. Should White roll a 2 next turn (other than 21 or 22) he will be forced to play 3/1*, exposing two more blots.

Meanwhile Black has a 42 to play and he should play 7/5, 6/2. Exposing the blot on the 2-pt has zero risk as Black still has a full prime behind it so White cannot escape. Next turn he will cover the blot and then the following turn he will hit White's blot on the ace-point and subsequently cover his own blot making a closed board.

This technique is called 'rolling the prime'. If at any time during this process he gets hit he just recirculates the hit checker and repeats the process until he is successful.

Back games can be long and complex and they require a balance of judgement, especially with regard to the doubling cube, and technique. However, remember the advice at the start of this section – don't play back games unless you are forced to do so.

Scrambles

So far the game types we have studied have been relatively easy to define. Scrambling is more difficult. It usually involves one side trying to 'scramble' home a loose checker – one that got hit during a mêlée somewhere on the board.

A typical example is shown below. In this position White is on roll. Black already has one checker back and will have another if White can roll a 1. Black's board is already a mess and may well deteriorate rapidly from here.

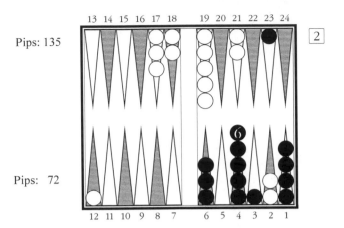

Pips: 135

Pips: 72

Many players as Black receiving a redouble here would drop and go on to the next game. In fact Black has a comfortable take. He has a number of things in his favour: his home board, at least for the moment, is stronger than White's (three points made to White's two); if the blot on the 3-pt is not hit it may soon become a four point board; he leads the race by 63 pips – that is a huge lead; White's checkers are not that well distributed. Of these factors the key is the race – Black can withstand quite a few setbacks before he falls behind in the race.

None of this means that Black is well placed but you would be surprised how often he can escape that last checker and bring it home safely. In fact Black wins nearly 33% of all games from this position. White has a variety of threats but he cannot carry them out all at once and all the while one good roll from Black, for example a 36, could put him in a powerful position. The vast majority of players would underestimate Black's winning chances in this type of position and invariably make the wrong cube decision.

Actually, White is not strong enough to redouble. He needs to improve his position before it becomes technically correct to redouble. Note that word technically – in practical play you must redouble positions such as this – remember Woolsey's Law. Quite often you will have to do no more than to add two points to your tally on the score.

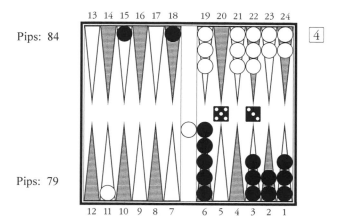

Pips: 84

Pips: 79

Here is a complex 'scramble' from a very important match. Black (John O'Hagan) led White (Dennis Carlston) 14-10 in the 25 point final of the 2005 World Championship. He is trying to scramble home his last two checkers whilst Carlston languishes on the bar.

The move he actually played, 15/10, 6/3 was reasonable but not quite the best. He should have played 18/15/10. This embraces two themes we have already looked at: connectivity – the last two rear checkers remain in contact with each other; duplication – Black duplicates the numbers, 4 and 5, which White needs both to enter and hit. Two rolls later Carlston hit the blot that O'Hagan had left on the 18-pt, won the game and tied the score at 14-14. From there he went on to win the World Championship.

This single, admittedly small, misplay may have cost O'Hagan the World Championship but such is backgammon – huge swings of fortune on a single roll. To my mind this sort of excitement and the adrenalin rush it can create are what make backgammon one of the greatest games in the world.

In this example we started talking about scrambling and ended up including connectivity and duplication. This is often the case. We have to include many different elements and techniques when analysing a backgammon game or position and the more experience we get the better we become.

In the calm of one's study after the game it is often quite easy to do this analysis but over the board it is a very different situation and that is why the best analysts are not always the best players.

Saving the Gammon

Sometimes you have to surrender the game and just try to avoid the gammon. Your sole objective is then to bring all your checkers into your home board as quickly as possible and to bear off at least one of them.

To do this you aim to move any checkers you have left in the outer boards to precisely your 6-pt. Only in exceptional circumstances should you waste any pips by bearing your checkers in any deeper than the 6-pt. You should also seek to get as many crossovers as possible with each roll as you bring your checkers around the board. You must optimise your chances of getting at least one checker off.

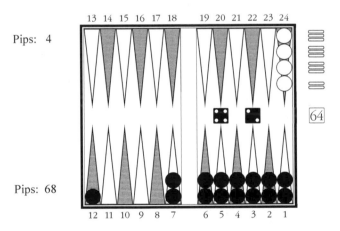

In this position Black could play 12/6, optimising the use of his pips but then, next turn, assuming White does not roll a double, Black will need a double of his own (6 rolls) to save the gammon. In this instance he has to waste pips but maximise crossovers with 7/3, 7/5.

Then if White doesn't get his double Black will have 15 rolls to save the gammon (any 6 plus 22, 33, 44 and 55).

The other key decision area in saving gammons is whether to stay for a late shot or run for home as quickly as possible.

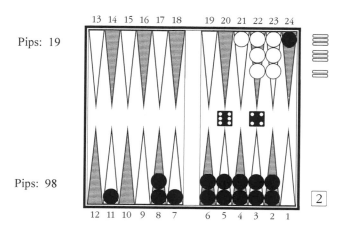

Pips: 19

Pips: 98

Here Black could run with 24/14, using all ten pips in the race to save the gammon, or he could play 11/5, 8/4, wasting three pips but hoping either to win the game or at least save the gammon by getting a late shot and hitting it.

After 24/14, Black will have to roll 20 more pips to bear a checker off (18 pips to bring the remaining checkers to his 6-pt and two pips to bear a checker off his 2-pt). We have seen that the average dice roll is just over eight pips. Therefore Black will probably need at least three and possibly four rolls to take a checker off. Meanwhile White with seven checkers left will need four rolls to take those checkers off but if he rolls a good double that will reduce to three rolls.

The upshot of this is that Black is not a favourite to save the gammon by running so he should waste three pips by playing 11/5, 8/4 and see what happens next roll. He can then re-evaluate his game plan based on what White rolls and on his own next roll.

Playing Technique

Having looked at all of these middle game types we are not quite finished. In the last part of this chapter we need to revisit how we actually play the game move by move. What I mean by this is: 'what are the thought processes that we should employ when it is our turn to move?' We examined this earlier when we looked at selecting candidate plays but now we are equipped to study this critical part of the game in much more depth.

Backgammon and Golf

If you study the top fifty golfers in the world you will find players with different temperaments, very different golf swings and slightly varying skill sets. However, they have one thing in common. Before each shot they go through exactly the same pre-shot routine. Again, the routines vary but the fact that they have one does not. You cannot be successful at golf without a pre-shot routine.

The same is true of backgammon - the best and most successful players have a pre-roll routine. They structure their approach to the game and know exactly what they are doing. Of course there are many other things that contribute to becoming one of the best players but like golf you cannot succeed without the preparation phase.

In backgammon we can take things one stage further because we need to combine the pre-roll routine with the post-roll routine - that is, the decision-making process that happens after we roll the dice. The two routines in combination create what I call the "Play Routine".

Play Routine

So what does a play routine look like? There are four elements, the first two pre-roll and the other two post-roll:

The Doubling Cube

- As we have seen, every roll is a doubling decision. The key question is to test whether there has been sufficient change in the position in the last two rolls (one by you, one by your opponent) to warrant cube action. Should you be doubling/redoubling?

- When you play a game you are not coming fresh to each position because you have the past history of the game in your mind. Therefore it is not a total re-evaluation each turn but rather you are just updating a known position.

- The other side of the coin is that you may be offered a double in which case you must go through the same process. Decide how much the position has changed since your last evaluation, apply your knowledge about the take/drop process and make your decision.

Plan

- Throughout a game you should always have a plan. This plan should be based upon the middle game strategies we have already discussed. For example you might be in a blitz and your plan should be to consider how to bring more checkers into range of your home board so that you can continue your attack.

- Unfortunately the dice do not always cooperate and you might not be able to execute your plan as required. Ask yourself, "can I still execute the plan I decided on last turn or have the last two rolls changed the position so much that I must change my plan?"

- The mark of a strong player is his or her ability to change plans according to circumstances. For example, if your blitz stalls because your opponent anchors in your board, then you might now be playing a mutual holding game and you will have to change your plan accordingly.

- Sometimes life is complex and more than one plan might be feasible. If so, try to keep your options open until the dice enable you to decide which option is best.

Candidates

- Having completed your pre-roll analysis you now roll the dice and have to identify the candidate plays. The question to ask is, "given my plan(s) and this dice roll, what are the possible moves that I can make that support this plan?"

- Sometimes this is easy but more often than not there will be at least two candidates to consider. Selecting candidates in the first place will be based upon your experience and knowledge and as a beginner you will miss candidates because your model of the game will exclude them. Here is a non-trivial example:

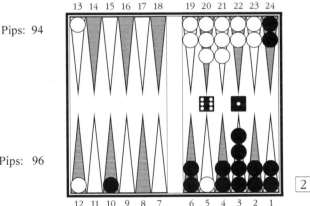

- Here the majority of players would move 10/4, 3/2 and hope for a miracle double 6 or to hit a fly shot (a fly-shot is one where you need both dice to achieve the hit; in this position 65 for Black played 24/13* would have been a successful fly shot).

- Only an expert would consider the candidate play 24/18, 6/5* (!!) which incidentally is the correct play in this position.

156

- Equally well an expert would not consider playing 13/6 with an opening 43 but a beginner may do so because he has not yet learnt the principle of taking risks in the opening phase of the game.

Select and Play

- Having established a list of candidates you now have to decide which amongst them is the best. Once again, this can be difficult and it is sometimes very easy to make the wrong choice. Success at backgammon is often measured by how few mistakes you make and, as you improve, so you make fewer mistakes because your understanding of the game has improved.

- Always remember that the rules of backgammon allow you to try out moves and your move is not completed until you pick up the dice. If you have a choice between two close plays then try them both – often seeing the resulting positions will help you make up your mind.

- Finally, make your move with conviction and pick up your dice.

Summary

Unlike golf, backgammon is played at a fairly quick pace so following this play routine during a loud and noisy chouette is never going to be easy but as Gary Player once said, "it's funny, but the more I practise the better I become".

One final point, when your opponent is on roll he will often stop to think because he is going through the process above. You can make good use of that time to think about the position so that when it becomes your turn to play you have already gone through some of the pre-roll routine.

Chapter 12: Chouette

Introduction

Not long after the invention of doubling in the 1920s the players of the day looked to create a version of backgammon where more than just two players could take part. Piquet (a card game) was quite popular at the time and a variant existed in which many played against a single player. This variant was known as 'chouette'. Whence the name? Chouette is the French for screech owl, a bird that is always attacked by all the other birds - as we shall see that is most appropriate for this form of the game!

Over the years the rules of chouette have evolved considerably. Here I am going to provide the rules most commonly in use today.

Chouette Rules

One player known as "the box" plays against the remaining players, known as "the team" or "crew", one of whom is designated as "the captain". Each team member has his or her own doubling cube. A team member may consult other team members about moves but only after either the box has taken the team member's double to 2 or after the team member has accepted the box's double to 2.

Until that first double the captain decides on the moves on his own (this speeds up the game considerably). Once consultation is permitted the captain still has the final decision about all moves in any case of disagreement.

The players rotate in strict order. Let us say that Player A is the box playing against B, C and D where B is the captain. If A wins the game he keeps the box, C becomes the captain and B goes to the bottom of the queue. If, however, B wins the game as captain he becomes the new box, C becomes the captain and A goes to the bottom of the queue.

What makes a chouette really fun is that each member of the team has his own doubling cube and must make his own cube decisions. This significantly increases the money involved. For example, in a four-handed chouette the box is playing against the other three players, and is in effect playing for three times the nominal stake. If he wins he gets a point from each player (assuming the cube has not been turned) but, if he loses, he loses three points.

Take for example a five-handed chouette and assume that the box has accepted a double from all the other four players. If he now loses a gammon that will cost him 16 points rather than the 4 point loss if he had been playing head-to-head. Losses in the box can be very expensive - one of America's top players recently claimed a world record by losing 300 points in a single game in a ten-handed chouette!

Whilst any one of the team can double at any time, another standard rule is that if the box offers an initial double he must offer it to all the team members at the same time.

It is not unusual in a chouette for doubling cubes to be found on both sides of the board. For example, let us say two of the team, B and C, decide to double the box whilst D decides to wait. The box takes the cubes, turns the game round, and then decides to double D who accepts. Thus the box has two of the cubes and one of the team members, D, has the other. This is just one example. Believe me doubling in chouettes can get very complex – I have been in five-handed chouettes where all four cubes have been at different values on each side of the board at the same time.

Once the number of players gets beyond five it is quite commonplace for the box to take a partner to spread the risk. Suppose A is in the box against B, C, D and E and furthermore that just as A loses the game, a new player – F, decides he want to join the chouette. This is easy to accommodate. B becomes the new box, A (the outgoing box) becomes B's partner and C becomes the new captain. When the box has a partner the same rules on consulting apply to them as to the team, that is, they cannot discuss moves until at least one doubling cube has been offered and accepted.

Observations and Advice

There are a number of advantages to chouettes. Firstly, they are the most social form of backgammon and a room with a big money chouette at its centre is never going to be quiet. It is thus a good way to meet new players. Provided a new player can afford the stakes he will always be welcome in a chouette - a bit like cutting in at bridge.

Secondly, for someone who is intent on improving his game, playing in a chouette with better players is ideal. Unlike many games where experts are loath to explain their reasons for making a certain play, in a chouette they have no option as they have to convince their captain of the soundness of their plays. If you can't take the financial risk of playing in a chouette, then listening and watching one for a few hours can be nearly as effective since you will probably learn a lot from the heated discussions that ensue. However, until you have actually played and learnt to cope with the peculiar pressures that chouettes can bring, you will not have learnt all the lessons.

Other than the final round of big tournaments, all of my most memorable backgammon evenings have come from chouette play. Here is an example:

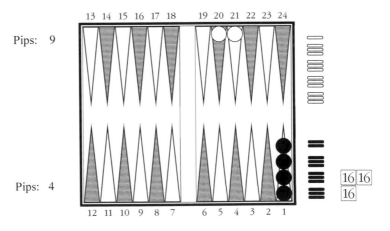

I was the box, on roll, and held three cubes on 16 and we were playing for £20 a point. In diagrams for chouette play all the doubling cubes are shown. It had been a really great game with the advantage changing hands several times. I redoubled to 32 and waited. Technically this is a drop. White wins only 23% of the time. I'll leave you to work out how I arrived at that figure – it's quite easy.

However, as you will find in backgammon in general and chouettes in particular, some players are loath to drop high cubes. I just happened to be playing against three of them so they all took. The cubes were now on 32. I rolled 43 and took off two checkers. Now they have 10 rolls that win and 26 that lose. The captain shook the dice for a long time and then cast them. The first dice came to rest on a 5. The second one spun interminably but finally it too came to a halt – on a 3!

£1,920 to me but one pip more and I would have lost. That was nearly a £4,000 swing on one roll of the dice – exciting enough for you?

Financial Management

A word of advice - don't play in a chouette unless you can comfortably afford to lose 150 times the nominal stake. That means if the nominal stake is £1 per point you must be able to write a cheque for £150 and then go home and sleep soundly. My own story above proves the point in dramatic fashion.

This is an example of how worrying about money can cause you to lose it:

161

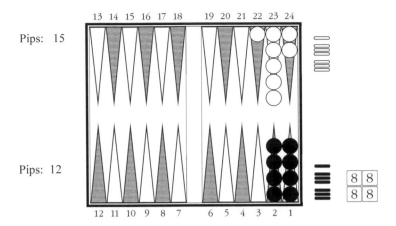

Here Black was in the box and owned four 8 cubes. It had been a roller coaster of a game.

Black did not double. He was worried about losing 64 points if things went badly. He wanted to wait a roll and then double out his opponents next time. It would be a 3-roll ending and they would have to drop. Sadly the team's double five scotched his plan. And the really sad thing? This position is already a redouble and a drop – Black's timidity cost him 64 points anyway (he lost 32 instead of winning 32).

How well a player performs during any one chouette is often influenced significantly by his score. Human beings do not always demonstrate rational behaviour as this simple diagram shows:

SCORE

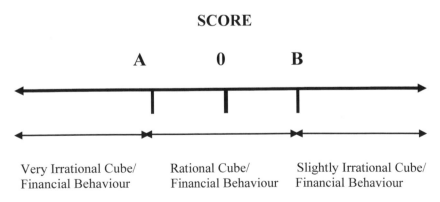

Players have a fascination for zero. Irrespective of how well they have played, if they finish plus for the night they are happy; a minus score leads to gloom and despondency.

In the diagram above, the line represents a player's score for the night where the centre point is zero.

- Between A (a minus score but not a huge one) and B (a plus score but not a huge one) rational cube and financial decisions are made.

- Once a player gets well ahead – any point to the right of B - then he will often tighten up. By this I mean that he doubles late to guarantee a win and he drops doubles that he should take for fear of losing a gammon and his nice profit.

- Conversely when a player gets a big minus score – any point left of A – he will do one of two things: drop more quickly than usual because he is fearful of going further behind or, much more likely, he will steam. 'Steaming' is a backgammon term used to indicate that a player is chasing his losses by taking doubles he should drop and doubling very early to make sure he doesn't lose his market.

Activating Consulting

One of the complexities of chouette play is that you are playing with – or against – a group of players who have their own personal styles and idiosyncrasies. It is vitally important to learn quickly about your fellow players. What is a clear take to one is a clear drop to another.

You can maximise your earnings by discovering weaknesses in your opponents and then adjusting your play accordingly. The main consideration will always be your evaluation of the position but it must be tempered by the human factors involved.

As we noted above, as a team member you may not consult with the captain until your cube has been turned, either by you or the box. If the captain is a strong player that does not matter too much but what if he is the weakest player in the game? The sooner you can give him some help the better.

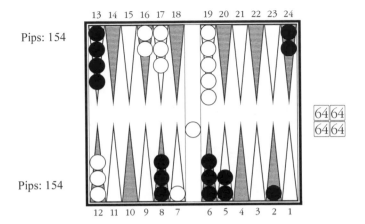

In the position above, the team is Black and White (the box) has just fanned. Black has the edge here but does not have enough to double yet. However, a weak player could well misplay this position and lose the advantage. With a weak player as my captain I might well venture an early cube here purely to activate my ability to consult.

I won't be giving away much if things go poorly and there are three prospective benefits: the position is gammonish so if the blitz (the indicated game plan) succeeds I will win four points; the box may drop my double to keep me out of the game so that I can't talk; if we win, the weakest player will be in the box – perfect!

Finally, in a chouette most players strive to get into the box. This is strange because the box is at a disadvantage. With one against many, the one will sometimes miss a play or an idea - the many rarely so. Therefore, let me pass on, from the legendary Paul Magriel, the most useful piece of advice on chouette play I have ever been given.

"90% of the time your games in the box will define your evening in terms of winning or losing. You are at a disadvantage so make sure you take a little extra time on each play, even if only a few seconds, and for doubling decisions ALWAYS take more time than usual."

Chapter 13: Tournament Play

Introduction

Whilst money play generates exciting backgammon, it is not as complex as tournament play where the match score brings an added dimension of difficulty. In money games each game can be considered as a stand-alone entity and the doubling decisions relate only to that single game. In a tournament game the match score is paramount, and a position that might be no double and a take in a money game can be a double and a pass at certain match scores. Strange things also happen when the cube gets to a high value in a short match.

Basics

However, I am getting ahead of myself. Let us cover the basics first. Backgammon tournament matches are always played to an odd number of points, typically 7 or 9 for short matches and extending to 25 for the final of the World Championships. A format growing in popularity is the best-of-three 9-point matches. This latter format is generally reckoned to be a better test of skill as an 8 or 16 cube can destroy even the best player's chances in a single 25-point match. I can find no reason for matches being to an odd number of points; it would appear to be purely historical.

Crawford Rule

In the first game after one player reaches match point, for example leading 6-2 in a match to 7, the doubling cube may not be used. This is known as the **Crawford Rule** and is named after the famous American master John Crawford who did so much to popularise backgammon in the 1960's and 1970's. His book, "The Backgammon Book" co-authored with Oswald Jacoby, provides a fascinating insight into the history of backgammon. The game with the Crawford Rule in effect is called the **Crawford Game.**

165

The reason for the Crawford Rule is that after one player reaches match point his opponent has no reason not to double on his first roll of each subsequent game - as he will lose the match anyway if he loses the game, but will win 2 points per game (or 4 if he wins a gammon) if he wins. Because this tactic considerably favours the trailing player, Crawford introduced his rule to try to redress the balance somewhat in favour of the leader. The rule quickly gained universal acceptance and I have never played in a tournament where it was not in use.

An oft-told anecdote is that of Walter Cooke, sadly now deceased, playing a kindly old Greek gentleman in a 13-point match at London's Clermont Club. Walter established a 12-1 lead. His opponent ground out the next three games to bring the score to 12-4. At this point Walter pointed out to his opponent that he should double on his first roll of each game as he had nothing to lose. The Greek thanked him and took the advice, winning two doubled gammons in a row to bring the score to 12-12.

At the start of the next game he proudly announced, "I don't think I need to double this one" and promptly went on to win the match. Bemused, Walter strolled over to the draw sheet to see who had benefited from his misplaced generosity, only to discover that the beneficiary was none other than Aristotle Onassis!

So remember, once the Crawford game is over, the trailer should double the leader at his first opportunity.

Jacoby Rule

The Jacoby Rule is never used in tournament play, and it is perfectly correct in many tournament situations to play on for an undoubled gammon with the cube still in the centre.

Automatic doubles, beavers and raccoons are never played in tournaments.

Free Drop

Note that in the first game after the Crawford game, if the trailer requires an even number of points to win the match, e.g. trailing 3-6 in a match to 7, then the leader can drop one double without costing himself anything. Thus, at 3-6 to 7, the trailer will still have to win two further games (excluding gammons) to win the match even after the leader has dropped a double. This is known as the **free drop** and should normally be exercised at the first opportunity.

If you lose the opening roll as leader then that is normally sufficient to justify using the free drop. If the trailer needs an odd number of points to win after the Crawford game then the leader must take all initial doubles. For example, if you are doubled when leading 6-2 to 7 you must take as the trailer will need to win three games to win the match (barring gammons). If you drop he will only need to win two more games.

Mandatory Redoubles

If the leader doubles when he is 2 points away from winning the match the trailer has a mandatory redouble. This is because if the trailer loses the game then he loses the match anyway so he risks nothing when he loses but gains considerably when he wins as he wins two extra points. Obviously this scenario is repeated where the leader is four points away from winning, holds the cube on 2 and redoubles to 4. Here the trailer has a mandatory redouble to 8 so the leader must be even more wary of giving the cube away.

Playing Style

The last basic point is that you must steer for certain types of game if you are leading and different types if you are losing. When you are losing you want to try and win gammons; when you are winning you try for simple races and holding games. This means you should vary your opening moves depending on whether you are winning or losing. If you are losing you should slot your 5-point with opening roles of 21, 51 and maybe 41. If you are winning you should use the 1 to split your back men. Similarly with 32, 43 and 54 you should bring down two checkers from the mid-point if you are losing but split the back checkers if you are winning.

Match Equity Tables

A warning – this is the most complex section of the book.

In the early days of tournament play the only difference between match and money play was that people were much tighter with the cube, and it was quite rare to see a 4 cube.

Gradually players began to realise that the score has a significant influence on cube decisions. Ideas such as not doubling so readily when ahead in a match became standard. Soon, some of the keener minds decided to work out match equity tables.

A match equity table gives the percentage chance of winning a match at any particular score. For example trailing 4-5 in a match to 7 points your chances are 41%; leading 7-3 in a match to 9 your chances are 81%. Three players, Robertie, Woolsey and Kleinman, derived their own tables based partly on mathematical theory but largely on empirical evidence. The three tables were approximately the same but did have some differences.

Over the years the method of constructing tables has become refined and the empirical evidence of real matches has greatly increased, so that there is now broad agreement on the table values.

Here is the match equity table for all possible scores in a nine point match given from black's perspective:

White Needs

Black Needs

	1	**2**	**3**	**4**	**5**	**6**	**7**	**8**	**9**
1	*50*	*70*	*75*	*83*	*85*	*90*	*91*	*94*	*95*
2	*30*	50	60	68	75	81	85	88	91
3	*25*	40	50	59	66	71	76	80	84
4	*17*	32	41	50	58	64	70	75	79
5	*15*	25	34	42	50	57	63	68	73
6	*10*	19	29	36	43	50	56	62	67
7	*9*	15	24	30	37	44	50	56	61
8	*6*	12	20	25	32	38	44	50	55
9	*5*	9	16	21	27	33	39	45	50

The important thing about the score in any match is not how many points have already been won or lost but how many points are required (or needed) by each player to win the match.

For this reason match equity tables are presented in a format that reflects just that. For example, if Black were leading White 5-3 in a match to 9 points that would normally be described as Black needs 4, White needs 6 or, in even shorter form, needs 4 vs. needs 6.

To get the correct percentage from the table we just find the entry for 'Black needs 4', 'White needs 6' and we see that the answer is 64%. The advantage of defining the table this way is that you can easily adapt it for shorter match lengths. For a seven point match we just need the first seven rows and columns.

The percentages in italics apply to the Crawford Game when one or other player is at match point. Match winning percentages for scores after the Crawford Game are not shown because the cube actions are trivial.

The problem is that very few people can remember tables like this although it can be done. Over the years various formulae have been derived to make the job easier.

I personally use the Janowski formula which is this:

Let D = The difference between the two scores
Let T = The number of points the trailer needs to win the match

The Leader's Winning Chances (W) are: $50 + \dfrac{(D \times 85)}{(T+6)}$

Trying this out on a score of 5-2 in a match to 9 we get W = 50 + 255/13 = 69.6%

This is very close to the value in the table and if we round up our answer we get the figure of 70% that appears in our table. Note that the Janowski formula does not work for Crawford Game scores – you will have to learn those off by heart.

Some people are not comfortable with the mental arithmetic required and in this case I would recommend investigating Neil's Numbers - a method derived by the American expert Neil Kazaross. Enter 'Neil's Numbers backgammon' into any Internet search engine and you will find the details.

Now let us see how understanding match equity tables can help us. Firstly let me say that in the early stages of a match, play and doubling decisions are likely to be the same as if you were playing a money game. It is only near the end of a match - or when there is a very high value cube - that things become different.

Examples

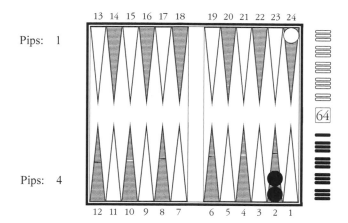

Pips: 1

Pips: 4

The above simple position illustrates the difference between match and money play. In a money game Black would double and White would take. In 36 games White would lose 26 games and win 10 for a net loss of 32 points - better than the 36 points he would lose by dropping. Therefore White would accept a double from Black.

Now suppose that Black leads White 5-4 (needs 2 vs. needs 3) in a match to 7 points. Again Black will double - should White take? Let us work it out:

- If White takes and Black throws one of his 26 (72%) winning rolls Black will win the match. If Black throws one of his 10 (28%) losing numbers then White will lead 6-5 with the Crawford game to be played. If we look at the table above we can see that White will then be a 70% favourite to win the match. From the position above, his chance of winning the match is the product of the likelihood of each event occurring, that is, winning this game and then going on to win the match. This product is 28% x 70% = 19.6%.

- What if White drops the original double? Then he will trail 6-4 with the Crawford game to be played. Again, from the table above we know that his winning chance from that score is 25%.

171

So if White takes he wins the match 19.6% of the time whilst if he drops he wins 25%. This is a huge difference and the answer is obvious - White must drop the double, whereas for money he would happily accept. Such a simple position but such a huge difference between money and match play.

Here is another classic match situation.

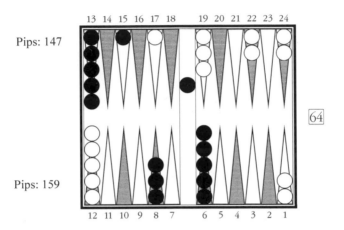

Black has opened with a 63, playing 24/15 and White has rolled 55, playing 8/3(2), 6/1(2)*. Black now rolls 63 and stays on the bar. Should White double, should Black accept? The answer depends on the match score.

First, as a benchmark consider the cube action in a money game. This is a well-known position where the correct action is double/take. Now we will suppose the score is 3-3 in a match to 7. In this instance White should double and Black should drop. Why should he drop?

The answer is because White is offering an optimally efficient double. If he wins a gammon - and a lot of his wins in this position will be gammons - then he will win 4 points, which is precisely what he needs to win the match. Black does better to decline and play from 3-4 down.

172

What if White leads 10-1 to 13? Then he should not double but should play on for an undoubled gammon. If White does double, Black will accept with alacrity and on the merest excuse redouble to 4. If Black then gets lucky he could even win a gammon making the match score 10-9.

Doubling Windows

In our discussion of races in Chapter 9 we introduced the concept of a Doubling Window. To remind you, the doubling window is the range of percentage winning chances where double/take is the correct cube action.

In a money game the doubling window stretches from 50% to 77% (approximately). The decision as to where in that window to double will be based upon the amount of play left in the game, the volatility, the gammon threat and, last but not least, the opponent. In a last roll situation the leader can double with any advantage.

In tournament play the doubling window is governed by the match score. A detailed explanation of doubling windows, their calculation and use is well beyond the scope of this book but if you become really hooked on the game and want to succeed at major tournaments then learning about doubling windows and their application will become necessary.

For now we will content ourselves with some general observations.

- At the start of a long match we have already noted that doubling decisions are normally as in money play.

- If one player establishes a substantial lead then his doubling window will shrink and in some cases virtually disappear. As an example, the correct cube action might be double/take only when the leader is between 80% and 84% favourite to win the game. Recognising that you are somewhere within that very narrow doubling window is highly unlikely. Often the leader loses his market in such situations.

- It is possible that it is correct to double or redouble when an underdog in a game. Let us suppose you trail 3-4 in a match to 7 and you hold the doubling cube on 2. Late in the game you have a shot. If you hit you will win the game but if you miss you will definitely lose the game. The necessary arithmetic will show that if you have at least a 30% chance of hitting – the equivalent of a direct shot – then it is correct to redouble to 4. Such a position is shown below:

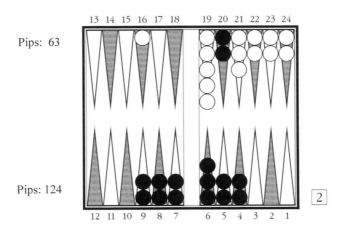

If Black rolls a 4, 13, 31 or 22 he will win the game but if he misses he will very probably lose the game. He should redouble to 4.

- The leader should be cautious about redoubling to 4 with a large lead – the cube will come flying back on 8 if the trailer even sniffs the chance of a win. Imagine losing a gammon with the cube on 8 – a 16 point loss would haunt you for a long time.

- The leader should steer for simple positions like holding games with low volatility and few gammon chances. Conversely the trailer should seek complexity, volatility and gammonish positions.

- The leader must be careful about redoubling, particularly towards the end of a match. Cube ownership is very valuable to the trailer.

- If the leader is doubled in the situation where he needs exactly the value of the cube to win the match then his take point is likely to be lower than 25%.

- When trailing by a large margin it is important to be aggressive with the cube. The last thing you want when trailing 1-10 in a match to 13 points is to lose your market in a gammonish position.

3-Away vs. 3-Away

Using match equity tables and doubling windows we can work out the optimal doubling strategy at many of the scores in a short match. I am going to mention just two of them.

At 3-Away (this is the same as needs 3) vs. 3-Away, that is, both players need 3 points to win the match, it is correct both to double earlier and drop earlier than in a money game. That is because the opponent needs at least a 30% chance to take the double.

2-Away vs. 2-Away

This is a score that often confuses beginners. At this score it is correct to double if there is any chance that you might lose your market by the next roll. Let us say your opponent opens with 62 played 24/18, 13/11. You must double. You might roll 66 played 24/18(2), 13/7(2)* and he might stay on the bar by rolling 66 – you will have lost your market.

From this you can see that between two players who understand this concept this will be the last game of the match as the cube will be turned within the first couple of moves.

175

Once the cube has been turned, cube ownership is valueless as are gammons and backgammons which brings us nicely to......

Double Match Point (DMP)

Double match point happens all the time in backgammon matches. DMP occurs when the cube is on a value where either player will win the match if he wins the current game. Trivially this happens when both players only need one point to win the match but it also occurs, for example, when the cube is on 2 at 5-5 in a match to 7.

At DMP, the only thing that matters is winning the game; gammons and backgammons are irrelevant. Lots of people forget this and play 'normally'. At DMP it is a good idea to play flexibly and keep your checkers in play if possible. Unless forced upon you by the dice, blitzes are not a good plan. The gammon that often results from a blitz is of no use and if the blitz fails your checkers are often out of position.

You even have to consider how you are going to play the opening roll. The latest thinking is that with rolls such as 32 and 43 you should make one of the splitting plays rather than bringing down two builders. With 64 you should run with 24/14 rather than play 24/18, 13/9.

Once you get into the middle game you must remember that the imperative is to win the game and that there is no need to play for a gammon. This means your game plan should be adjusted accordingly. Here is a very clear example of that idea:

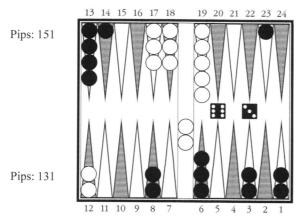

Pips: 151

Pips: 131

For money (assuming White has been doubled) and at some match scores the correct play is13/7, 13/10 trying to blast White off the board with a blitz. At DMP the right plan is to ensure that the last rear checker escapes without any problem. A blitz is still a possibility but getting that last rear checker on its way home is the priority. The right move is 23/14, escaping the rear checker completely. 23/20, 13/7 is also reasonable.

Flexibility is the key at DMP. A final piece of advice – if you are the better player, steer for complexity. The game can never be ended with a double and the longer it goes on the more chance your opponent will have to make a mistake.

Clocks

To enable tournaments to run on schedule we are increasingly seeing the use of clocks to eliminate slow play. Each player is allowed a number of minutes for his match (normally two minutes per point so for a 7 point match a player would be given 14 minutes) – this time is known as his bank. In addition he is allowed (usually) 12 seconds to make each move and only after those 12 seconds have elapsed is any further time used deducted from his bank.

As in chess, if you run out of time you forfeit the match. This can lead to some interesting tactics towards the end a match. As an example, a player whose opponent is very short on time will try to play a complicated game, for example a back game, with a large number of moves, in order to use up his opponent's remaining time.

Summary

This is a complex chapter and yet it has only scratched the surface of a very difficult topic. I would recommend re-reading it a couple of times and then trying to put the learning points into practice.

Don't worry if you found match equities initially too difficult. If you employ the more general concepts contained in this chapter you will be ahead of many of your opponents and you can leave match equities until you become more experienced.

Chapter 14: Computers

The Problem

One of the reasons that backgammon was slow to develop after the invention of the doubling cube in the 1920s was that it was very difficult to determine, or agree, what was actually the best move in any given position except late bear-offs. Backgammon theory was based purely on empirical evidence. For many years we took the word of the acknowledged experts of the day – after all they were the experts.

Early Computers

Then the bright young men and women of the 1970s developed the concept of rollouts. Surely if we took a position and played the game to conclusion enough times (rotating the first roll to allow for the 36 possible rolls of the dice) we would get an idea of the 'correct' play?

Yes we would and this was certainly better than anything that had gone before. Hand rollouts significantly improved our understanding of the game. The problem was accuracy. To get a reasonably accurate result (from a statistical perspective) required hundreds, if not thousands, of rollouts and we simply did not have the time.

Just when everyone was getting really frustrated, computers came to the rescue. The Personal Computer (PC) had arrived just in time to assist in the development of the game. Early attempts to create a backgammon-playing computer met with a modicum of success.

In 1979 Hans Berliner created the 'Gammonoid' program that (luckily) beat the then world champion Luigi Villa. However that program ran on a mainframe computer and it would be another 13 years before the first PC program arrived.

179

This was Tom Weaver and Tom Johnson's "Expert Backgammon" which ran on both Macintosh and PC. Whilst not great this program was a huge step forward and crucially, not only could you play against the program, but it included a rollout facility. You could feed it a position and ask it to roll out (hundreds of times) your chosen moves. Gone were the long tedious hours spent rolling out positions by hand. Whilst we slept computers could do the work. This was a huge step forward for backgammon.

"Expert Backgammon" was based on the same type of theory as most chess programs. Take a position, look at all possible future moves, evaluate those resulting positions and select the best one using a predefined algorithm.

This approach worked well for IBM's "Deep Blue" in 1997 when it beat the then World Chess Champion Gary Kasparov, but it was not quite so effective for backgammon. The problem with backgammon is that after a couple of moves there are so many possible variations that even the most powerful computers cannot look far enough ahead (in a reasonable time) to determine the 'best move' in any given position. This was frustrating but just when all seemed lost a new technology arrived.

Neural Networks

In the early 1990's in the IBM labs in White Plains, New York, a scientist named Dr. Gerry Tesauro began playing around with neural networks. Without going into the theory too deeply, the idea was to produce a computer that could more accurately model the human brain in its working. The approach would be to give the computer the basics of a problem and then let it work on the solution rather than giving it clear directions.

For Tesauro, backgammon was the perfect testing vehicle. He taught his program "TD-Gammon" the rules of backgammon and then told it to work out for itself the best strategy and tactics. It did this by playing half a million games against itself. By 1994 it was ready to meet the world.

180

The end result was fascinating as some of the plays that humans had thought for decades were correct were shown to be errors. That TD-Gammon was no mug was quickly proven when the best players of the day could only show a slight edge when playing long sessions against it. The game of backgammon had changed forever.

Not long after TD-Gammon came the first commercial neural net backgammon program, JellyFish, created by Frederik Dahl of Norway. Jellyfish was so named because in comparing its brainpower to that of humans it was roughly equal to a jellyfish. That is not to denigrate JellyFish - the program was a huge step forward for backgammon and it had a good user interface that made it easy for thousands of players to use.

Suddenly the overall strength of backgammon players took a big leap forward as more and more began to use and learn from JellyFish. Now, at last, rollouts could be relied upon for many types of position and humans were quick to learn from their silicon friend. JellyFish was by no means perfect and its handling of back games in particular was poor but as Neil Armstrong would say "it was a giant leap for mankind".

Next out of the blocks was Snowie (1998), the brainchild of Olivier Egger in Switzerland. It started life as "Snow White" but that caused problems with Disney and hence the change of name. Why Snow White or Snowie? Unlike JellyFish which has a single neural net, Snowie has seven (the seven dwarves) and it is consequently more powerful. Snowie was improved over the years with each new release, both in playing strength and user interface.

The one drawback to Snowie, and it is a big one for many players, is the price. At around the £200 mark for the Professional Version (the one that enables you to do rollouts) it is out of the reach of many of the very people who would love to have a copy.

Luckily, not long after Snowie appeared, the GNU Project, which is supported by the Free Software Foundation, decided to produce a neural net program for backgammon. This, not surprisingly, is called GNU Backgammon or gnubg for short. (For those who wish to know, the abbreviation GNU is a recursive acronym standing for "GNU's not Unix".) It was originally launched in 2002.

Like Snowie it has gone through many iterations and the current release is a very powerful beast indeed. Both Snowie and gnubg can hold their own with the very best players in the world. There are still technical areas of the game where they need to improve but they never suffer from the distraction of emotional influence and this gives them a huge edge over the vast majority of human beings.

We were promised Snowie 5 for many years but it never appeared and the word now is that it never will. Development of gnubg has also been suspended, at least for the time being.

Luckily there is a new kid on the block, eXtreme Gammon (XG) which is now in its second release (XG2) and is undoubtedly the strongest backgammon playing computer program of all time. Importantly for the backgammon community, it is also very affordable. XG is now the 'de facto' standard for the game and it is used by all serious analysts.

A term that is commonly used for backgammon computer programs is **'bots'** which is short for robots.

Using Computers

How do we use computers to improve our play? There are two very different ways, (a) playing against the computer and (b) using the computer to analyse a particular move or match.

Playing against Computers

When we play against other human beings we do not analyse our moves or record our games. With computers you can do both if you so wish. Playing against a computer is quite different and requires a little bit of getting used to. Your moves are all made using a computer mouse or the touch-screen technology of the iPad and similar tablet computers. On the computer screen you can have the board in a two or three-dimensional representation. Personally, I prefer the 3-D aspect but it is a purely individual choice.

When you first change from using a real backgammon board you will tend to overlook possible plays. This is simply part of the learning process – the more familiar you are with using a computer the less likely you are to overlook plays.

Nearly all computer programs will play at different strengths that can be chosen by the user. Most of them will have at least five playing strengths from novice through to expert. How does the computer vary its playing strength?

It does this by varying how far ahead it tries to look. It does this by a recursion method named 'Plies'. A 1-ply evaluation means the evaluation is the direct result of the neural network. Making a 2-ply evaluation means that the computer will, for each of the 21 possible rolls, take the following actions:

- Check the best move
- Evaluate in 1-ply the resulting position

The 21 results are then gathered and averaged (with a weight of 2 for a non-double and 1 for a double). This average is the 2-ply evaluation of the position.

For any subsequent depths, the system is the same: an n-ply evaluation is the average of all (n-1)-ply evaluations of the 21 possible rolls.

Obviously a 2-ply evaluation gives better results than 1-ply, and 3-ply is stronger still. Modern computers do not really have a problem with playing at 3-ply levels because they are so powerful. In the early days of computing you could have made and drunk a cup of coffee whilst a 3-ply evaluation of a single move was going on. With XG we now have the option of doing 4-ply and 5-ply evaluations and no doubt in time software developers will add more ply, though we may reach the point of diminishing returns.

When you play against XG, or other programs, there are various modes of play available. For example you can play in 'tutor mode' so that the computer will give you hints when you make mistakes or you can play in tournament mode where it will give you no help whatsoever.

The computer will keep a record of your game as it progresses. The following diagram shows a snapshot of a game after just a few rolls using XG. The board is in 3D display mode:

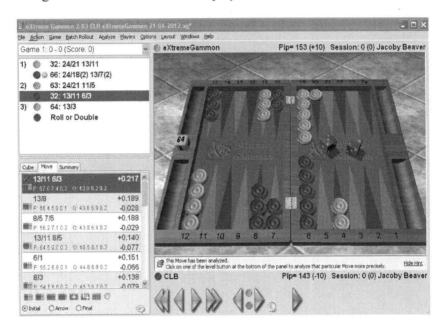

The diagram contains a wealth of information including, very usefully, the pip counts for both players. The log of the game so far is shown on the top left-hand side. The position is shown for the move highlighted which in this case is Black's play of 32.

In the bottom left-hand corner XG shows an analysis of Black's possible plays of the 32, ranking the moves from best to worst, based on equity. As you can see the move chosen, 13/11, 6/3 was the best move possible.

In this last paragraph I have introduced the word equity. What is equity? This is a term I have deliberately avoided mentioning until now but this is a convenient moment to define a term that is commonly used in backgammon and other games.

Equity

- A player's equity in any given position is simply an amount – the amount, in points (irrespective of the stake), which the player expects to gain or lose on average if the game is played to completion from that position.

- In an even game a player's equity is zero; on average he expects neither to win nor lose.

- If a player is certain to win and he is playing for one unit his equity is +1. If he is certain to lose his equity is –1.

- If a player is certain to win a gammon and he is playing for one unit his equity is + ? If he is certain to lose a gammon his equity is –2.

- If a player is certain to win a backgammon and he is playing for one unit his equity is + 3. If he is certain to lose a backgammon his equity is –3.

- In any situation the two players' equities sum to zero.

- All of the above refers to what is called 'cubeless equity'. However, if the doubling cube is in play, its location and value both affect the equity. The resulting 'cubeful equity' of a player can, as a first approximation, be determined by multiplying his cubeless equity by the value of the doubling cube.

What about if a player is 75% favourite to win a game – what is his cubeless equity? It is simply the difference between his winning chances and losing chances. In the 75% case that is 0.75 − 0.25 = 0.50.

This gives us a useful reference point in terms of equity − in any given position if a player's equity is close to 0.50 he should at least be considering doubling and conversely the opponent whose equity is −0.50 (remember the two players' equities always sum to zero) will know he might have to think about whether to take a double.

Thus in our game position above, XG tells us that after the move 13/11, 6/3 Black's equity is 0.217 so he is not in doubling territory but, crucially, do not forget that White has yet to roll and his move will change the equities before it is Black's turn to play again.

Incidentally, a roll that is very good and substantially increases your equity is known as a **joker** and one that dramatically decreases your equity is an **anti-joker.**

Back in the 1970s and 1980s equity was a term only occasionally used in backgammon but since the advent of computers and their use of it to express winning/losing chances it has become commonplace.

A player's equity is complicated by the possibility of winning a gammon or a backgammon. This makes the equity calculation more difficult but luckily the computers do that for us.

In our example XG has evaluated the position using 3-ply analysis. You can ask it for evaluations at different levels − the higher the level, the more accurate the answer (but the more time it takes).

One final point from our example: the difference between the best play and the second best play is an equity difference of 0.028. Any equity difference between two moves greater than 0.03 is rated as an error and any difference greater than 0.08 is classed as a blunder.

Learning from the Machine

How do we use all this information? When you play against a computer you should follow the normal thought processes and decide on your move. If you want to check your intended play against what the computer thinks, you can press the hint button. Often you will choose the same move but the learning process begins when your move is different from its evaluation.

Then you should stop to ask yourself why. At first you may not always know the answer but gradually you will begin to understand the game in more depth and appreciate the computer's choice. Because they are so powerful, computer programs are right more often than not and the big step forward comes when you begin to incorporate their 'thinking' into your own play.

The strength of backgammon players is measured by their error rate which is calculated by how often and how much their chosen moves and doubling cube actions differ from those selected by the computer. Expert players very rarely make blunders and naturally make fewer errors than the average player.

Rollouts

While computers are fast they are not yet all-powerful and so even they cannot examine each move to their maximum capability in real-time play. As we have seen above they will play to a certain ply depending upon the level set by the user.

To truly analyse a move, or set of moves, in any given position, human beings long ago established that the best way to do this was to roll out the game to the end and record the result. This would be done at least 36 times - one for each possible initial roll of the dice - and then the results would be averaged.

The problem then becomes one of statistics – how many times do you have to roll out a position to be reasonably sure, from a statistical viewpoint, that the answer that you have obtained is the correct one?

The answer, in non-scientific terms, is very many. This book is not meant in any way to be a statistics manual so we will shortcut to the answer and the software solution. Many thousands of rollouts are required for statistical comfort. That explains why, when humans attempt to gain meaningful data, they can never do enough to be sure whether the answers they have obtained are correct. Luckily, the computer experts have devised ways to ensure that the likes of XG can produce good results from a relatively small number (but still large in human terms) of rollouts.

All I will say here is that the technique employed is called 'Variance Reduction'. If you would like to know more you will need to study neural net technology in some depth. The end result is that by performing something like 1,500 rollouts (and quite often a smaller number will suffice) we can arrive at the best move – or cube action – for any given position. These 1,500 rollouts can be done in a matter of minutes on a standard PC. Common practice is to set up the program to do a series of rollouts and then while you sleep the PC happily does the analysis. You can study the results when you awake in the morning.

Here is an example of a rollout in action:

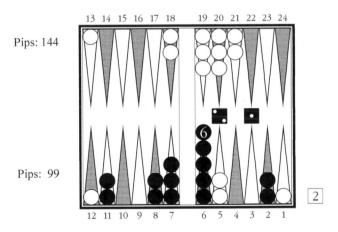

Pips: 144

Pips: 99

This position is from one of my own games - I was Black. I had been doubled early but had turned the game round although I had an ugly stack of six checkers on my 6-pt. I decided that, because of the strength of my opponent's home board, I would play safely with 8/7, 8/6 and hope for something better on my next roll.

188

The other possible moves I considered were 11/8, starting to clear my 11-pt, and 6/3, slotting my 3-pt and hoping to make the point on my next turn if my opponent didn't hit the blot

I went on to lose the game. Had I been cowardly in playing 8/7, 8/6 or was I just unlucky? I put the position into XG to see what its opinion was. I initially did a simple 2-ply evaluation.

Here is XG's initial assessment:

6/3		**+0.417**
P: 59.4 9.5 0.1 O: 40.6 7.7 0.2		
11/8		**+0.349**
P: 55.0 10.3 0.2 O: 45.0 7.2 0.2		**-0.068**
8/7 8/6		**+0.335**
P: 55.7 11.4 0.1 O: 44.3 8.9 0.1		**-0.082**

It ranked the move that I played, 8/7, 8/6, as third best showing it as a blunder with a negative equity difference of 0.082. The tick against the play indicates that this was the move played in the game.

(A brief word here on the second line of information shown for each move.

This provides XG's estimates of the number of single games, gammons and backgammons that each player will win. Thus in the diagram above the player making the move (P) will win 59.4% of the games with 9.5% of those wins being either a gammon or a backgammon and 0.1% (of the 9.5%) will be backgammons. The other three figures show the same percentages for the opponent (O).

A further discussion of how to use this information and other statistics provided by XG is beyond the scope of this book. However, if you really want to improve your game I suggest you take the time to get a good understanding of the program. XG's online help guide is a good place to start.)

However, I was not satisfied and so I set the program to roll out each of the three possible plays. This next diagram shows the results:

8/7 8/6	+0.425
P: 59.1 8.4 0.1 O: 40.9 7.9 0.2	
6/3	+0.418
P: 58.3 9.4 0.2 O: 41.7 9.1 0.3	-0.007
11/8	+0.351
P: 54.6 10.8 0.3 O: 45.4 8.6 0.3	-0.074

As you can see XG, with a more in-depth analysis, has changed its mind and its number one ranked play is now 8/7, 8/6 although it only just edges out 6/3. This confirmed my own analysis during the game and provided me with a new reference position. When I come across a similar problem in future this reference position will help me to decide whether I should play safely or take some risk.

Using Rollouts

This is the primary use of rollouts. They enable us to learn from our mistakes and thus improve our game. The way to learn even more from rollouts such as that above is to change the position slightly and see if the rollout result changes. For example, if one of White's checkers on his 4-pt was on his 8-pt, thus weakening his home board, would the recommended play still be 8/7, 8/6? The answer is no, because the slot is now less dangerous and 6/3 becomes the correct play. So with a little bit of work we get two new reference positions for the price of one.

Quite often in backgammon we make the 'right' move but end up losing the game. When this happens in a chouette the loss can be both expensive and annoying. You can take away at least some of the pain by checking your play in a rollout. If you made the best move and lost then you must accept it as part of the game – at least you are likely to sleep better. If you made the wrong move you will hopefully learn from the rollout and not repeat the mistake.

At the next level of detail you can study the percentages of single games, gammons and backgammons won and lost and learn how some plays can lead to more gammons but fewer total game winning chances and vice versa. This is especially important when studying positions that occur at Double Match Point when gammons do not count. We have already seen that the play at a certain match score may be different from the play in a money game. We can use rollouts to educate us in this area of the game as well.

Playing against computers and using rollouts to help analyse your play accelerate progress along the learning curve and it is certainly possible to become a very good player in one to two years instead of the eight to ten years that it used to take (on average).

I recommend using rollouts as often as possible to improve your game.

Backgammon Apps

When I wrote the original version of this book Steve Jobs had yet to launch the iPad and tablet computers were in their infancy.

In the intervening five years the world has moved on and the use of smartphones, iPads and tablet computers is now commonplace. I sometimes wonder how I ever managed before I had an iPad.

Developers have produced a plethora of backgammon apps for Apple and Android devices. Typically these apps can be used to play against the computer program itself or against other players over the Internet.

Using these apps is yet another way to improve your game. Because a device like the iPad is so portable and its touch-screen interface so good you can easily practise your game when travelling to work on a train or bus or when just relaxing at home.

For some time "Backgammon NJ" was my iPad app of choice. It is a very strong player and has lots of useful features. For example, you can play a match against it, email the details of the match to yourself and then use XG to analyse your play, thus combining the best of two types of computer play.

However, as this book goes to press XG Mobile has just been released. I was lucky enough to be involved in the final stages of testing the app. It is truly excellent, both in playing strength and user interface. One very useful feature is that you can input any position and get an instant evaluation of either the best move or the correct cube decision – it could become an invaluable aid in chouettes to help settle arguments! You can also export your games so that you can do more in-depth analysis using its big brother, the full PC version. My strong recommendation is to invest in XG Mobile. Like the PC version it will quickly become the de facto standard for the game. In due course there may well be an Android version as well.

I have no doubt that the apps will get stronger and more sophisticated over time and I look forward to making more and more use of them. Another useful backgammon app provides the facility to record positions, and there are also a number of apps that can turn your iPad into a backgammon clock.

Chapter 15: Online Play

History

It may surprise you to learn that people have been playing backgammon on the Internet since 1992. Needless to say, the experience in 1992 was vastly different from what is available today.

Back in 1992 the Internet was in its infancy and it would be five years before most of the world would come to recognise it. However, some intrepid early pioneers were already using it, although in fairness it has to be said that it was extremely difficult and many hours were wasted trying to get it to work. I should know - I was there.

In the backgammon world Expert Backgammon (the first PC program) had just become available so players were getting used to the idea of playing against computers. In the 1990s the backgammon scene was relatively quiet and often players had to travel significant distances just to get a game.

To overcome the problem Andreas Schneider created FIBS (First Internet Backgammon Server). For the first time players could compete online. As you would expect, the user interface was quirky and there were connectivity and cost issues (remember having to use dial-up and being charged by the minute?).

However it was an immediate success and was enthusiastically embraced by the backgammon community. For the first time players could be accurately rated based upon performance using the ELO method first used in chess. In ELO terms 1,500 is an average player, 1,800 is a strong expert and 1,900 is a master.

FIBS was the only significant online site for five years but, once the Internet saw 1000% growth in 1997, other companies began to enter the market. The Internet of 1997 was light years ahead of its 1992 cousin and program user interfaces were much better. The first new site out of the blocks was GamesGrid and because of its excellent interface it soon attracted the best players. Back in 1997 most people were still hesitant about buying things over the net but backgammon players seemed to be the exception and the secure payment system of GamesGrid worked well from the outset.

Since then things have moved on considerably and the biggest change came about when broadband arrived. This solved three problems of the early days almost immediately: the cost of connectivity was on a flat fee basis so staying online for hours at a time was no longer an issue; the speed of play was increased so the experience could be just like playing over the board and connectivity became much more stable so it was very unusual suddenly to find that your opponent had vanished.

Now there are a large number of online backgammon sites and that number is on the increase. Because there are so many I am not going to point you in one specific direction. (To obtain a list of current online sites use the Chicago Point weblink included in the Bibliography). Rather I will provide advice and guidance about how to play on the Internet and some of the things that you should look out for when selecting where to play. Before I do that I need to cover one other important topic.

Cheating

In online poker you cannot use computer programs to assist your play. Poker is a game of hidden information. Your hole cards in Texas Hold'em are known only to you and the same is true for your opponents; thus cheating becomes nigh on impossible. Backgammon is a game of total information. In other words all the information is visible to both players. This makes the use of an artificial aid that much easier.

One of the concerns of online play has always been that unscrupulous players would use a bot such as XG to "assist" their play and indeed this has happened from time to time. To combat this possibility the online sites developed software that can quickly detect patterns of play that indicate someone is cheating and instances of malpractice are now rare.

You can never completely eradicate the possibility of cheating but it is becoming harder and harder for the cheat to prosper. The backgammon community quickly punishes, via ostracism, anyone caught using underhand tactics.

Playing Online

Preparation and Enrolment

Before playing online I strongly recommend playing against a computer program so that you can get used to the user interface. Each online play site has its own unique features but in the main the look and feel of Internet play is very similar to playing against XG or Snowie.

There are certain things that are common to all online sites:

- You will need to register by providing a user name and password.

- For some sites you will have to download some software to your PC. Most of the newer sites allow you to play through a standard browser and either method is acceptable.

- A small number of sites require a subscription.

Use recommended websites and choose between playing for money and playing for fun. If you are going to play for money you will need to deposit some money in your online account.

Starting Out

Whatever site you join I recommend that you only play for fun initially. We will look at playing for money shortly. There will be thousands of players who will be happy just to play with you without any thought of profit. They play purely because they enjoy the game and they want to improve. Until you are comfortable with the user interface and more importantly your own skills you should continue to play for fun.

You can choose to play single games, a series of games or a match of an agreed length. I recommend starting with a number of single games, then a series and then progress on to playing matches. Short matches of 3, 5 or 7 points are ideal. They can be completed in a relatively short space of time and provide an excellent learning vehicle for understanding important scores such as Double Match Point.

Nearly all sites have a resident bot that you can play against for free so take advantage of that as well.

Chat

A key element of all good online sites is the chat feature. This enables you to converse with your opponent while you are playing. What you chat about is up to you; normally it is about the game but you may also exchange personal information as well.

Unless you specify otherwise your game (or match) will be visible to anyone else logged on the site. The spectators may also join in the chat unless they are specifically barred from doing so by the players.

Chat provides a tremendous way to learn about the game and if you choose matches being played by strong players then the chat will be particularly informative. As backgammon becomes more popular and the Internet more pervasive, many top tournament finals are broadcast live on the Internet.

If you are lucky some of the world's top players will watch the match from the comfort of their own homes and provide a running commentary. As an example, Neil Kazaross, who is one of the world's best players, kept thousands of players enthralled with his chat commentary on the 2006 World Championship final between

Luigi Villa and Philip Vischjager. Anyone lucky enough to have been online during that match got a superb free lesson on how to play tournament backgammon.

Money Play

Once you are happy with the basics you can progress to playing for money. Again, the same formats are available, single games, a series of games or tournament play. Be careful to play for small stakes initially and make sure that you are holding your own against players at the level at which you have elected to play. For example if you are consistently winning at $1 per point then you are probably ready to progress to the $2 or $5 game. Conversely if you find yourself losing consistently then you need to move down a level.

It is not universally true that the bigger the stake the better the player but in general that is the case. Take care not to play for too large a stake too early in your career. In the days before the Internet sometimes the only way to develop one's game was to play in a chouette where the stakes were more than one could really afford. That situation is no longer valid as anyone can now develop his or her game at very lost cost by selecting the right level of play online.

In nearly all money games you play for a stake per point, for example $5, but you also set an upper limit on how much you can win or lose in any one game. If you are playing for $5 per point you might set that upper limit at $20, i.e. four times the nominal stake, or possibly $40, eight times the nominal stake. This very sensible method acts as a protection against very high cubes and helps you to manage your money.

I would say that in the majority of online money games four times the nominal stake is the norm. This limit gives rise to some interesting doubling situations that don't arise in normal over-the-board play. I will give an example to demonstrate my point:

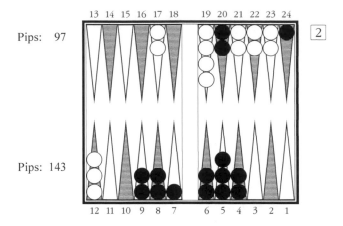

Let us assume that as Black you are playing for $5 per point with an upper limit of $20 for any one game. Early in the game you doubled but things have not gone well and now White redoubles you to 4 – should you take or drop?

In an unlimited game, although you will win from this position fractionally more than 25% of the time, you also lose quite a few gammons which sadly means that you have to drop the redouble.

In our limited game things are different because losing a gammon won't cost you any more than losing a single game. With the doubling cube on 4 you will lose $20 if you lose the game. If you lose a gammon, which would normally cost you $40, you still only have to pay out $20 because of the loss limit.

Thus a position that would be a drop in a normal game becomes a take in this online version. Note also that if the game should turn around again Black will not be able to win with a subsequent redouble to 8 as the stakes have already reached their maximum and a further redouble would be meaningless. So, to accept redoubles in situations like this, the taker needs 25% (or more) winning chances in order to accept a redouble.

Ratings

Once you begin to play in money tournaments on some sites you will receive an ELO rating that we discussed briefly above. After you have played a few matches this ELO rating will provide you with a good estimate of your playing strength. Importantly you will be able to see the ELO rating of your opponent so that you can make sure you are not playing someone out of your class.

Having said that, it is always good to play against better players so don't be discouraged from playing against someone within 100 rating points of yourself but once the gap gets to 200 or 300 then take care.

Tournaments

Once you are familiar with matches then the final step is to enter a tournament to test your skills. Most tournaments are simple elimination events. A field of 8, 16, 32 or 64 enter at a specified cost, $50 for example, and then play each other using a simple knock-out formula until the winner emerges.

The higher the entry fee the better the players and, of course, the better the prizes. In a large tournament the semi-finalists, runner-up and winner will receive prizes. In an eight- player tournament it will be winner takes all.

In tournaments your losses are limited to the entry fee but your potential winnings could be quite lucrative. In an eight-player $50 tournament (sometimes known as a jackpot) the prize will be $400 (but see the section on costs below) so your profit would be $350.

Ideally you should combine online play with live play. Recently the hybrid tournament has emerged following poker's lead. A number of qualifying (or satellite) tournaments are held on the Internet where the prize is free entry into a major live tournament with all expenses paid. This model is becoming increasingly popular. For the cost of

$25 you could win through to play in a live tournament where the prizes could be in the thousands of dollars.

Costs and Payments

The online sites are doing a tremendous job in promoting the growth of backgammon but they are also there to make money for their owners. As such they charge a fee (or rake) on all money games. For pure money sessions they will charge a very small percentage of the agreed stake per game and at the end of each game the costs will be deducted from the winner's profit.

Similarly for tournaments the operator will take a small percentage of the entry for 'the house'. In the example above, the winner of the eight-player tournament may actually win $375 rather than $400 because of the administration fee.

Some sites seek to protect weaker players by charging a higher rake for games between players of very different ratings. This is done to deter strong players from preying on beginners and players less skilled than themselves. In poker you are advised to look round the table for the sucker and if you can't see one then you are probably the sucker yourself. In backgammon weak players playing out of their depth are known as 'pigeons'; the predators are known as 'sharks'.

Site Features

There is really very little difference between the many online sites and at any point in time one may be more popular than its competitors. When choosing a site to use, here are a few things to consider:

- Has it been recommended to you by colleagues?
- What is the subscription model (if any)?
- Are you comfortable with the user interface?
- Do strong players use the site? (Helpful from the point of view of learning.)

200

- Are there players from all levels so that you can always get a good game no matter what time of day it is?
- Does it, by repute, have a good cheating detection system?
- Does it sometimes add additional prize money to its tournaments (over and above the entry fees)?
- Does it have a good support system?
- Does it pay winnings promptly?

Summary

Online play is rapidly changing the face of backgammon and I am sure it will evolve considerably during the rest of this decade. The online chouette is surely not far away. As already noted, you can develop your game rapidly by playing online where time and space set no limits – you can play 24 hours a day against people of all nationalities. Backgammon is a truly international language.

Chapter 16: Where to from here?

In the foregoing chapters I have covered everything you need to know in order to start playing the game of backgammon. I hope you have enjoyed the journey so far despite the odd foray into arithmetic.

In truth you can play the game at the level that feels comfortable to you. Many people have played all their lives and never done a pip count and would not give house room to a match equity table. These players have probably taken just as much pleasure from backgammon as many a world champion.

I have provided enough information for you to choose the level at which you want to play and it is up to you how much time and effort you devote to the game. If you just want to play on the beach whilst on holiday, that's fine. Equally well, if you really get hooked on the game, the knowledge that you have acquired through reading this book will give you a solid start on the road to becoming an expert backgammon player.

One thing is certain – you do not become an expert overnight but, with the advent of computers, it can be achieved much more quickly in this century than the last. I have played the game for over thirty years and with the availability of Snowie, XG and online play I have played nearly every day for the last five years. I am still learning about the game and I know that like all great games it can never be completely conquered but I'm doing my level best to improve.

Having got this far what do you do next? Here are my suggestions:

- Re-read this book until you are comfortable that you have a firm grip on the fundamentals of the game.

- Start to play with family and friends. If possible play in a small chouette so that you can listen to the exchange of ideas.

- Join one of the online play sites and play just for fun or for very low stakes that you can easily afford.

- Watch matches between experts on the online sites and study the chat as the games progress.

- After a while think about playing in a live tournament. Alternatively, or in parallel, start to play matches online.

- If you can, find a local backgammon club and join it.

- Study further by buying more advanced books. My personal recommended reading list is shown in the Bibliography section of this book. Unfortunately many advanced backgammon books are expensive because they have small print runs but, let me assure you, they are well worth the price.

- Backgammon can now be found on TV. Watch these programmes whenever you have some spare time.

If you follow these suggestions you will have every chance of becoming a strong player. Please remember, however, that backgammon is a dice game and that no matter how hard you try there will be evenings when nothing goes right. You make all the right decisions but everything seems to go against you.

The Double Fives was London's premier backgammon club for many years and not long after it opened we were graced by a visit from Paul Magriel who at the time was certainly one of the top five players in the world. Paul managed to lose £1,500 to one of the weakest players in the club. Being the gentleman that he is, he merely raised an eyebrow, paid up and left. In subsequent visits over the next two months he won ten times what he had lost on that first night thus proving that the better player will always win in the long run.

We have all heard backgammon hard luck stories so here are a couple to finish with.

The first one is my own from a chouette during the British Championships in the early 1990's. A couple of rolls before this position occurred I had redoubled all four players to 8 and was surprised (and pleased) to get four takes. When we reached this position I was just thinking that with a high double my gammon chances would look quite good. At £20 per point that would be £1,280.

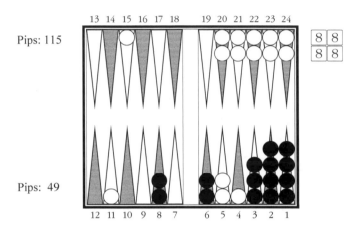

Pips: 115

Pips: 49

I rolled the dice and out popped 63! I had to play 8/2, 6/3 leaving two blots and a quadruple shot. My opponents gleefully redoubled to 16 and I had to drop. There was a £1,920 swing on that one roll of the dice. Surprisingly enough, I did not sleep well that night.

However, this pales in comparison to the coup that Paul Lamford pulled off against a player who shall remain anonymous.

In this position Paul (playing Black) threw 66 and entered three checkers from the bar by playing bar/19(3), 19/13:

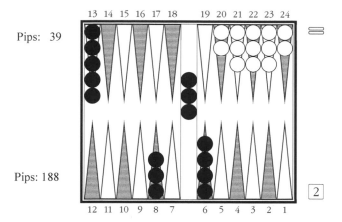

White already has two checkers off. If Black is really lucky he will save the gammon about once every 10,000 games. Paul actually won this game! Whilst he rolled ten successive sets of doubles his poor opponent averaged less than 3.6 pips per roll. Paul calculated the odds of Black winning as 1 in 10 to the power of 39. If it can happen, then one day it will.

Once you learn to cope with losing from positions like the two we have just seen then you will become a much stronger player. If you let the loss of one game affect you for the whole evening then you are on a downward spiral. As the great bridge player Bob Hamman once said, "The only important hand is the next one". Apply that thinking to backgammon and you won't go far wrong.

Finally, let me just mention that backgammon is extremely addictive. I fell in love with the game many years ago and I still have the passion for it now that I had in the late 1970s. Backgammon distorts time. Whilst eight hours in the office can drag interminably, eight hours at the backgammon table slips by in an instant.

Many years ago I lived in New York and decided one Saturday evening to go to the cinema. I had three hours to kill so popped into my backgammon club at about 4 p.m. Twenty-seven hours later, and all of $15 richer, I wondered if I might catch the Sunday evening showing of the film. Luckily, common sense prevailed and I took myself off for a well-earned rest.

You have been warned!!

Bibliography

There are many backgammon books, albeit many of them are only available from specialist stockists. What follows is my personal list of essential reading and many of them have been referred to in this book. Study these and you will truly become a much better player:

Title	Author(s)
Backgammon	Paul Magriel
Advanced Backgammon – Volumes 1 & 2	Bill Robertie
Modern Backgammon	Bill Robertie
Classic Backgammon Revisited	Jeremy Bagai
New Ideas in Backgammon	Kit Wollsey & Hal Heinrich
The Backgammon Encyclopedia – Volume 1	Kit Woolsey
How to Play Tournament Backgammon	Kit Woolsey
Backgammon Boot Camp	Walter Trice
The Doubling Cube in Backgammon – Volume 1 *(note: this book is currently out of print but occasionally comes up on eBay)*	Jeff Ward
Vision Laughs at Counting with Advice to the Dicelorn	Danny Kleinman
The Backgammon Book (extended version)	Oswald Jacoby & John Crawford
What Colour is the Wind?	Chris Bray
Second Wind	Chris Bray
Wind Assisted	Chris Bray
Backgammon Praxis – Volumes 1 &2	Marty Storer
What's Your Game Plan?	Mary Hickey & Marty Storer
Improve Your Backgammon	Paul Lamford
Sports Psychology – The Key Concepts	Ellis Cashmore

The quote from Kit Woolsey on "Woolsey's Law" is taken from "Inside Backgammon" which was a superb backgammon magazine that was produced by Bill Robertie and Kent Goulding and published from 1991 to 1998. It is no longer available but copies can sometimes be found on eBay.

Websites

There are many backgammon websites and online play sites. With the latter there is constant change and therefore I have not listed specific sites. The Chicago Point links portal is the most comprehensive backgammon website and from there you can find any other backgammon site. It maintains an up-to-date list of online sites and also has links to all things backgammon from history to equipment to lists of backgammon clubs and forthcoming tournaments. It also contains links to XG, Snowie and gnubg. It can be found at:

http://www.chicagopoint.com/links.html

Made in the USA
San Bernardino, CA
20 April 2014